A Student's Guide to Open Science

A Student's Guide to Open Science

Using the Replication Crisis to Reform Psychology

Charlotte R. Pennington

 Open University Press

Open University Press
McGraw Hill
Unit 4
Foundation Park
Roxborough Way
Maidenhead
SL6 3UD

email: emea_uk_ireland@mheducation.com
world wide web: www.mheducation.co.uk

Executive Editor: Beth Summers
Editorial Assistant: Hannah Jones
Content Product Manager: Ali Davis

A catalogue record of this book is available from the British Library

ISBN-13: 9780335251162
ISBN-10: 0335251161
eISBN: 9780335251179

Library of Congress Cataloging-in-Publication Data
CIP data applied for

Typeset by Transforma Pvt. Ltd., Chennai, India

Praise Page

"'A Student's Guide to Open Science' takes the reader on a journey to (and through) the world of open science with care, clarity, and creativity. It is essential reading for anyone who wants to make sense of open science, by covering complex content in an accessible and hands-on way. My hope is that every psychology student will finish their degree with a heavily annotated, well-thumbed copy of this important and timely book!"
Dr Madeleine Pownall, University of Leeds, UK

"The last 10 years have been a whirlwind in psychology: identification of faulty research practices, frequent failures to replicate findings, research on how the field could improve, and adoption of new solutions to make research more transparent and credible. It is a lot to take in, and it is hard to know where to start. I am frequently asked to recommend a reading that provides an overview of what has been learned during the last 10 years and a gateway for getting started with open science. With this book, now I have an answer. Dr Charlotte R Pennington has pulled off a remarkable trifecta of being clear, concise, and comprehensive in covering the origins of the open science movement and practical advice for adopting the behaviors. Moreover, she brings high credibility to others entering the field with her own story of getting started and becoming a leader in the open science movement. If you want to develop knowledge and skills for doing rigorous and transparent research, start here!"
Brian Nosek, Executive Director, Center for Open Science, Professor, University of Virginia, US

"Written by an inspirational early-career leader, this is a complete and accessible guide to everything open science, from the history of the replication crisis through to current, practical solutions and – crucially – how to implement them. This book will equip future generations with the tools necessary to improve our disciplines, and thereby represents a significant ray of hope for the future. Essential and timely."
Dr Emma Henderson, University of Surrey, UK

"This book provides a comprehensive and optimistic overview of how research practices have improved in the last decade. It will inspire and educate the next generation of researchers to contribute to science done right. The idea that students will start their scientific research with the knowledge and toolset presented in this book fills me with excitement about the future of my science. Every bachelor student should read 'A Student's Guide to Open Science' before their first research project."
Daniël Lakens, Associate Professor at Eindhoven University of Technology, The Netherlands

Dedication

To my teacher, Mr Pickwell; you sparked my passion for psychology, and your enthusiasm motivated me to pursue an academic career.

Contents

List of Figures

List of Tables

Acknowledgements

Many people have influenced my learning of the topics in this book, through excellent research articles and critical (but importantly, friendly!) discussions. I want to thank the following people who have contributed to my academic development personally: Dermot Lynott, Chris Chambers, Kate Button, Andrew Jones, Priya Silverstein, Loukia Tzavella, Kait Clark, Daniël Lakens, Sam Westwood, Flavio Azevedo and Emma Norris. Madeleine Pownall, Jackie Thompson, Helen Nuttall and Helena Hartmann also belong on the above list but deserve an extra shout-out for providing helpful feedback on chapters of this book. I'd also like to thank the fantastic members of the *Framework for Open and Reproducible Research Training*, the *UK Reproducibility Network* and *ReproducibiliTEA* for being sources of inspiration and support, as well as fantastic role models. Thank you to my friends and family for putting up with my musings on psychology and reminding me to 'have a day off'. And finally, to my partner Daniel for filling my life with love, laughter and happiness.

I mainly wrote this book in an independent and sustainably sourced coffee shop named 'Method' (oh, the irony!). It's thanks to their chilled vibe, incredible music and kick-ass coffee that I finished writing this book!

1 Introduction

Throughout high school, I had never been very good at mathematics (or so I thought) and used to tell myself 'You can't do it!' whenever I was asked to solve a maths problem. During my undergraduate degree in psychology, I came across the phenomenon of 'stereotype threat' and remember thinking that all of the questions and doubts about my maths ability had been answered. Steele and Aronson (1995) coined this term to describe how knowledge of widely known societal stereotypes (e.g. 'women are bad at mathematics') creates a self-evaluative threat that has a disruptive effect on performance. In a series of what are now considered 'classic' studies, they showed that simply telling Black students that their performance was indicative of race-related ability was enough to make them underperform on standardized tests compared to their White peers. However, when these students were told they were completing the same test to measure psychological factors related to verbal ability, performance was equivalent between both racial groups. Extending these findings, Spencer et al. (1999) found that women underperformed when they perceived a maths test to be confirmative of gender differences in mathematical ability; yet they performed similarly to men when this negative gender–maths stereotype was dismissed before the test. These studies were hugely influential in the field of social psychology and beyond because they offered a situational explanation for educational attainment gaps. The theory was persuasive and relatable: many of us belong to at least one group characterized by a negative stereotype, and this theory could explain how this impacts us individually.

As a student, I vividly remember reading articles detailing the findings of multiple experiments with unambiguous results and found myself believing that this could explain my own experiences in high school. The published literature gave the impression that stereotype threat was a completely robust and entirely reliable phenomenon: hundreds of studies demonstrated the stereotype threat–performance relationship across a wide range of groups and domains, in both the lab and the field (e.g. Barber et al. 2015; Beilock and McConnell 2004; Beilock et al. 2006; Skorich et al. 2013). So, a few years later, feeling convinced and passionate about this colossal body of work, I chose to expand on it as the topic of my postgraduate research. In 2013 I eagerly set out to pursue a *PhD* in experimental social psychology. My thesis aimed to build on prior work to uncover the mechanisms underpinning the stereotype threat–performance relationship (Pennington et al. 2016), with a view to developing interventions to reduce academic achievement gaps (but I never quite got to the second part!).

Throughout my PhD, I continuously refined my experiments and tried to replicate previous research, but I couldn't routinely demonstrate the predicted effects: in many of my studies, the experimental group performed similarly to the control group, and I reasoned that my tasks were introducing ceiling effects (a measurement limitation that occurs when the task is too easy and cannot discriminate performance differences). I felt like a failure. How could other researchers be publishing studies with seemingly perfect findings that detected these effects time and time again? What was I doing wrong to *not* find support for my hypotheses? I tried to publish my research, but the null findings made things very difficult. Other researchers in the field who reviewed my work suggested that my findings did not contribute anything to the literature, and recommended I run more studies to hone in on the effects. I worried endlessly about my academic career; I knew I needed publications to succeed in a competitive job market (as per the 'publish or perish' culture of academia – see Chapter 3) and was told by many that these should be in 'high-impact, prestigious' journals. In some of my experiments I got lucky, and for many others I continued to submit the null findings until eventually they were accepted for publication. But these academic pressures, coupled with my apparent failings as a researcher, affected my well-being. I was anxious, I lost weight and I found myself sleeping more and more. I felt very low. Looking back on these times, I wish I had known what I know now: many of the published studies in the older social psychology literature are just *too good to be true*.

In 2016, I heard about this thing called the ***replication crisis***, and strangely, just like in the early days with the theory of stereotype threat, I felt like all of my questions had been answered. I had joined Lancaster University as a Teaching Associate and my office was opposite that of an academic named Dr Dermot Lynott. Dermot had covered his office door with stickers relating to the replication crisis. The term ***replication crisis*** describes the widespread difficulty and failure to reproduce results of published studies in large-scale replication attempts (Pashler and Wagenmakers 2012). This is also referred to as the '***reproducibility crisis***' and, more positively, the '***credibility revolution***' (Munafò et al. 2017; Vazire 2018). This was the turning point through which I became interested, albeit a little overwhelmed, by the monumental problems facing the field of psychology. Many of the findings that I had come to love, trust and be inspired by throughout my undergraduate studies were not replicable and, as you will see in Chapter 2, the field of social psychology was faring particularly badly.

I started to read more deeply into the events that sparked this 'crisis' and found that scepticism concerning the theory of stereotype threat was increasing. Over the years I would learn how this literature was plagued by ***publication bias*** (Flore et al. 2018; Shewach et al. 2019; Zigerell 2017), and how independent research teams found findings either inconsistent with the original theory or could not replicate them at all (Finnigan and Corker 2016; Flore et al. 2018; Gibson et al. 2014; Moon and Roeder 2014). None of these challenges were mentioned in social psychology textbooks or taught in my degree, but thankfully these initial replication attempts helped me to understand that it was *not just me*: I was not the only one who was finding it difficult to detect stereotype threat effects, and I was not a rubbish scientist after all! I felt betrayed and almost lost my passion for psychology. I questioned whether to continue pursuing an academic career.

But from the ashes of the replication crisis, something interesting evolved. Something that would reignite my passion and convince me to continue pursuing my dream career as a researcher. That something was **open science**. Dermot encouraged me to join Lancaster's Open Science Working Group and I got involved in two Registered Replication Reports – studies that aimed to replicate classic findings on social priming (McCarthy et al. 2018; Verschuere et al. 2018). Because only three researchers could lead these projects at a single institution, Dermot stepped down and offered his place to me (a true sign of a wonderful mentor). It was through these two events that my enthusiasm for open science took hold. **Open science** (also referred to as 'open research' and 'open scholarship') reflects the idea that knowledge of all kinds should be openly accessible, transparent, rigorous, reproducible, replicable, accumulative and inclusive (Parsons et al. 2022). Subsumed under this umbrella term are many practices that work towards these goals, such as study preregistration, open materials and data, and open access publishing, as well as wider conversations about equity and representation (see Chapters 4 and 5). In my view, open science allows the discipline of psychology to improve its research practices and provide a roadmap for other disciplines facing similar issues.

I am now a Lecturer in Psychology at Aston University in Birmingham and have changed research fields to study addictive behaviours (I suppose I was lucky because I'd studied this as a side-line to my PhD). I teach about the replication crisis and open science at any chance I get, and I would shout about it from the rooftops if I could! But I also reflect on how daunting it was to learn about psychology's (recent) history and all of the new terms and practices that open science brings with it. This fast-paced movement is changing the face of psychology as we know it, and it sometimes feels difficult to keep up! This is why I wanted to write this book. With my experiences in mind – my early years of wrestling with stereotype threat and my later years of learning about the replication crisis and open science – I wanted to write a book that I wish I could have read when starting out. A book that educates people about the problems that psychology and many other disciplines face, that dispels the sense of imposter syndrome that we *all* feel when learning new topics, that promotes the wonderful world of teaching and research as a career, and that encourages you to be the best researcher, or consumer, of research that you can be. Open science can reform psychology because, at its heart, lies *transparency*.

An overview of this book

This book aims to provide a comprehensive examination of key events that sparked the replication crisis in psychology and an overview of open science practices that may offer the solution to improving replication and reproducibility. The book is split into six chapters. In this first chapter, I have told you a little bit about myself and my challenging experiences as well as introducing some key terms that will be explained in detail later in the book. Setting the wider scene, Chapter 2 provides a recent history of the replication crisis in psychology, outlining key concepts and discussing whether the problems our discipline faces can really be conceptualized as a '*crisis*'. In Chapter 3, I outline explanations for the crisis, exploring academic incentive structures that underpin researchers' careers and 'Questionable Research Practices' that undermine the credibility of scientific findings. Chapter 4 then introduces open science as a solution for the problems that research disciplines currently face, and summarizes its main practices, new initiatives that have emerged through large-team collaborative efforts, and emerging evidence regarding both the advantages and challenges that open science brings.

To help you put these practices *into* practice, Chapter 5 provides a 'how-to guide' on implementing open science – whether that be learning as a student, researching as a scientist or teaching the next generation of budding psychologists. Here I will outline the initial steps to creating a detailed study preregistration and Registered Report, provide some top tips for article preprints, and for sharing materials, code and data. Finally, Chapter 6 concludes with a summary of each chapter and an optimistic look towards the future as psychological science travels onwards through the replication crisis and into its next era of open science.

Who is this book for?

This book is aimed primarily at students studying psychology at both undergraduate and postgraduate levels. It aims to act as a springboard for more in-depth learning of open science and the implementation of best practices. After all, as psychology students you represent the grassroots generation of researchers who can learn from its murky history and improve the discipline further (and in Chapter 4 you will see how many open science initiatives have been spearheaded by early-career researchers!). In addition, this book should prove useful for educators teaching about these topics, who are free to utilize the pedagogical activities in their teaching. I also include some shiny new empirical evidence that is hot off the press! Finally, this book may be enjoyed by the general public who are interested in finding out more about psychology, the challenges this discipline faces, and the many solutions that have been put in place to solve them.

How to use this book

The core concepts of research underpinning this book are taught in research methods and statistics modules, particularly in psychology teaching. Therefore, some of the content I introduce to you may not be new and you will recognize some familiar concepts along the way. However, the replication crisis and open science are not yet taught commonly in universities, and are either completely missed or only briefly discussed in psychology textbooks! While I believe that this will change in the years to come, this book represents (to the best of my knowledge) the first student-centred textbook that not only teaches these topics, but also provides a handy guide that can be used in students' own research projects and assessments. Please engage with this book in whatever way makes the most sense to you and your journey; you may want to read it from cover to cover and immerse yourself in open science, or you may want to keep it nearby as a reference book when you're learning about research skills in your degree. Either is fine! I've written this book to be read flexibly and encourage you to dip in and out throughout your learning.

Some pre-emptive warnings

Throughout this book, I will use the terms 'replication crisis' and 'open science' and focus predominantly on psychological research. However, it is important to note that replication concerns are not an exclusive feature of psychology: many other scientific disciplines, such as cancer biology, artificial intelligence and economics, are also facing similar issues (see Begley and Ellis 2012; Baker 2016; Camerer et al. 2016; Hutson 2018). Disciplines such as particle physics, in contrast, appear to have developed many different initiatives that are aimed at helping to ensure the credibility of their findings (Junk and Lyons 2020). Students and researchers of these specific fields may therefore want to read and follow the citations of these articles. Given my research expertise, I will also focus mainly on **quantitative,** experimental research rather than **qualitative** research. This is not to say that some of the issues discussed do not apply in equal measure to qualitative research – transparency is required for all areas of scientific inquiry. While reading this book, you might come across certain terms that are unfamiliar or complex at first glance. In each chapter, I therefore format some terms in **bold** and *italics*, which are either followed immediately by their definition or act as a signpost to the glossary at the end of this book. Finally, reading this book will not automatically make you a good researcher – you have to do that for yourself. Instead, I hope this book will provide a starting point to take what you want from the 'open science buffet' (Bergmann 2018) and return to the table to keep filling up your plate. Remember, we are *all* students of open science!

2 The replication crisis

In Chapter 1, I explained my own experiences as a PhD student in experimental social psychology, and my evolving passion for understanding issues in research and exploring open science as a solution. In this chapter, I will lead you through a recent history of the replication crisis and some important key events that have changed this discipline. I'll begin by discussing psychology as a science and examining how it should be practiced, before moving on to explore how we came to find ourselves in a replication crisis. Finally, I will take a critical look at what 'failures' to replicate mean, and whether or not psychology really is in 'crisis'.

Psychology as a science

Imagine picking up a tasty apple from your kitchen counter and placing it in the palm of your hand. Now, let go of the apple. What happens? You will find, every time, that the apple drops to the floor. Imagine repeating this experiment with your friend – you both take an apple and then, at the same time, let go. Does your friend's apple drop to the floor? By repeating this experiment, you have performed a *replication*, and a successful one at that! You have found support for Isaac Newton's theory of universal gravitation.

Replication is the cornerstone of science (Dunlap 1926; Lakatos 1978; Popper 2002 [1959]). For us to know whether a finding is real (and not a fluke), we need to repeat it and confirm that the results can be found again. **Replicability** can be defined as obtaining consistent results across studies aimed at answering the same scientific question, each of which has obtained its own data. The term replicability is often contrasted with **reproducibility**, which can be defined as obtaining consistent results when the *same* data are analysed using the *same* techniques (National Academies of Sciences, Engineering, and Medicine 2019). These two terms can, at first, seem difficult to tease apart, so let's envisage them in practice. To perform a replication, you would go into a lab and repeat your own or someone else's experiment, collecting new data to see whether the original results hold on repeated tries. To then reproduce these results, you would rerun the same analytical tests on your data to see whether you get the same numbers (or, historically, calculate these statistics by hand – thank you computers!).

We can see the importance of replication in writing about the philosophy of science. The **scientific method** dates back to the fifteenth century (Sir Francis Bacon, 1561–1626) to provide logical, rational problem solving across scientific fields. It is a process for experimentation that is used to explore observations and answer questions about the world (and for psychology, human behaviour). The scientific method can be conceptualized through five main steps, as shown in Figure 2.1. Scientific inquiry starts with an *observation* followed by developing a *question* about what has been observed. It then involves formulating *hypotheses* and testing these through rigorous *experiments*, before forming a *conclusion*. Importantly, the findings from each experiment should be *replicated* – only after one, or several, successful replications should a result be recognized as scientific knowledge.

Figure 2.1 The five steps of the scientific method, with replication as the cornerstone

Let's have a look at quotes from some of the most renowned philosophers of science and experimentalists which exemplify the importance of replication (note that the term repeatability is used interchangeably with replicability here):

> The proof established by the test must have a specific form, namely, repeatability. The issue of the experiment must be a statement of the hypothesis, the conditions of the test, and the results, in such form that another experimenter, from the description alone, may be able to repeat the experiment. Nothing is accepted as proof, in psychology or in any other science, which does not conform to this requirement.
>
> (Dunlap 1926)

> Only when certain events recur in accordance with rules or regularities, as in the case of repeatable experiments, can our observations be tested – in principle – by anyone. We do not take even our own observations quite seriously, or accept them as scientific observations, until we have repeated and tested them
>
> (Popper 2002 [1959]: 45).

From this, you should see that replication is essential for psychology to be taken seriously as a science. Unfortunately, as I will show in this chapter, we seem to have got lost somewhere along the way. Psychology has lagged behind the physical sciences, in which researchers routinely replicate studies from their own and other labs (Dennis and Valacich 2015; Junk and Lyons 2020; Schmidt 2009). This has arguably led to a literature in which many previous psychological findings cannot be taken at face value. But before we take a look at the issues unearthed in psychological science, let's first deepen our understanding of replication – there are two main *types* of replication, each serving a different purpose.

The first is known as an ***exact replication*** (also 'direct replication'). In this form, researchers aim to exactly recreate an original study based on its research questions, hypotheses, methods, context, treatments, and analyses. Take our initial example of the apple falling to the floor; for this to be classified as an exact replication, your friend (the independent researcher) would need to ensure that the apple was the same type, weight and size, and drop it from the same height. The second type is known as ***conceptual replication***. Here, researchers test the same research questions or hypotheses, but use slightly different measures, treatments or analyses, or assess whether the results hold under different conditions, such as context or time (Nosek and Errington 2017; Open Science Collaboration 2015). Take the apple example again: in the original experiment, you might have dropped the apple from a great height, but in a conceptual replication you might try dropping a different object from the same height or the same object from a lower height. One of the easiest ways to remember these two definitions is to zoom in on the first terms – an *exact* replication aims to do the *exact* same thing, whereas a *conceptual* replication tests the *concept* in a slightly different way.

Both types of replication are extremely important. Exact replications inform us about whether an original finding is likely to be a true effect, or whether it may have been a ***false positive*** (Type I error). This allows us to test, redefine or develop more robust theories. Conversely, conceptual replications help us to identify under which conditions the results hold. This allows us to assess the generalizability of such theories and their boundary conditions (e.g. a phenomenon might only be seen in a certain subgroup of individuals or in a particular context).

What science should be

We have therefore established that for psychology to be a science, it should adhere to the principles of replication and reproducibility. If an effect is real and robust, any researcher should be able to find the effect using the same procedures and an adequate sample size. Now let's turn to what else science *should* be:

- *Credible* – Science *should be* credible and not *in*credible. Scientists *should be* willing to have any claims and discoveries fairly scrutinized.
- *Trustworthy* – Scientific results *should be* reported accurately. The general public *should be* able to trust the findings they read and use them to make informed decisions.
- *Transparent* – Science *should be* crystal clear. Scientific methods and results *should be* reported in detail, allowing for independent replications, evaluation and cumulative knowledge.
- *Accessible* – Science *should be* accessible to all. Other researchers and the general public *should be* able to access, read and evaluate scientific findings easily.
- *Inclusionary* – Science *should be* diverse and inclusive. Scientists from under-represented groups *should* have equal participation and opportunities.
- *Collaborative* – Science *should* maximize the use of available resources and researchers *should* work cooperatively, rather than competitively, to produce high-quality work.
- *Self-correcting* – Science *should be* based on accurate evidence in the pursuit of knowledge. Errors found in articles *should be* corrected and explained, and this *should be* normalized as part of the scientific process.

But now I want you to close your eyes and imagine a stereotypical scientist. What do they look like? What are they doing? And how do they behave?

Now I will tell you what I see. I see a White man, middle-aged, standing in a laboratory with a big sign that says, 'KEEP OUT!'. His findings are precious to him, and he does not want anyone else coming in and looking at what he is doing. He does not want anybody to steal his blue-sky ideas. He does not want anybody to replicate his work or try to reproduce his findings. It's his science, not yours. This science is not transparent. This science is not accessible. And this science is not collaborative. In Chapter 4, we will find out about many wonderful changes that will hopefully dispel this stereotype. But my point is this: science is supposed to work in a certain way, with replication and reproducibility at its heart, yet it has not always been practiced in this way. Up until 2012, replications have been rare in psychology, and still to this day they are not valued in the same way as novel experiments. Perhaps if we had valued replications all along, we wouldn't find ourselves in a *replication crisis*.

A recent history of the replication crisis in psychology

A cascade of events influenced what is now commonly referred to as the replication crisis in psychology. This term can be defined as the finding, and the related shift in academic culture and thinking, that a large proportion of scientific studies *do not replicate* (Parsons et al. 2022). What do we mean by 'do not replicate'? Usually, when a researcher or independent research team reruns an original study and obtains the same result, we call this a 'successful' replication. On the other hand, when an attempted replication finds different or **null findings**, we label this a 'failed' replication. There are many different reasons why a study may or may not replicate, which we will explore in Chapter 3, but to fully understand why the replication crisis came to be, we first need to travel back in time to the key events that sparked it. Figure 2.2 provides a summary.

Figure 2.2 Landmark events in the history of the replication crisis

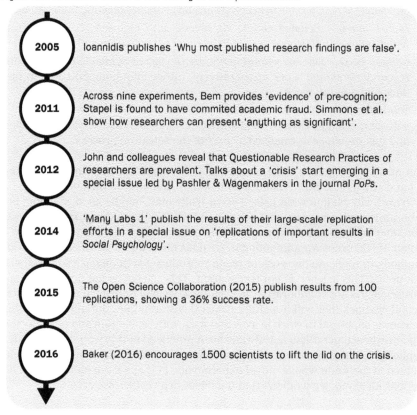

2005	Ioannidis publishes 'Why most published research findings are false'.
2011	Across nine experiments, Bem provides 'evidence' of pre-cognition; Stapel is found to have commited academic fraud. Simmons et al. show how researchers can present 'anything as significant'.
2012	John and colleagues reveal that Questionable Research Practices of researchers are prevalent. Talks about a 'crisis' start emerging in a special issue led by Pashler & Wagenmakers in the journal *PoPs*.
2014	'Many Labs 1' publish the results of their large-scale replication efforts in a special issue on 'replications of important results in *Social Psychology*'.
2015	The Open Science Collaboration (2015) publish results from 100 replications, showing a 36% success rate.
2016	Baker (2016) encourages 1500 scientists to lift the lid on the crisis.

Event #1: 'Most published research findings are false'

The first landmark event that caused a stir in the general scientific literature was a 2005 article by scientist John Ioannidis, which exclaimed 'why most published research findings are false'. In this article, Ioannidis claimed that many of the findings from his field of medicine and epidemiology were **false positives** (Type I errors). False positives lead a researcher to conclude that there is an effect in the population when this effect does not exist. Ioannidis argued that some of the main reasons for this stem from an overreliance on small, underpowered sample sizes, a preoccupation with p-values to denote **statistical signifi-cance**, flexibility in research design and analyses, and competition among researchers to produce positive results in fashionable research areas. Through data simulations, he demonstrated that when these factors are considered, most claims in medicine and other scientific fields are more likely to be false than true. Ioannidis' article crystallized the scientific community's awareness of the replication crisis well before the discipline of psychology realized it was in one itself. Future events would have us rereading this article with deep reflection.

Event #2: Could Bem 'feel the future'?

What if I said that you could predict the future with higher-than-chance certainty? That you were, indeed, psychic? Would you believe me? Well, in 2011, a psychologist named Daryl Bem wrote an article that convinced the world that undergraduate students could! In this article, Bem (2011) detailed the results of nine experiments with over 1000 participants that seemingly evidenced precognition – the phenomenon whereby people's conscious awareness of *future* events can influence *current* ones. Yep, you read that correctly: according to this theory, what happens to you next week could likely have caused what happened to you yesterday.

The studies were quite simple, but with mind-blowing results. Bem took four well-established psychological effects and 'time reversed' them so that the causal stimulus occurred *after* participants' responses to the event had already been recorded. In one of Bem's experiments, participants were first shown 48 words from four categories and were asked to memorize each word. Then, participants were asked to recall as many of these words as they could – a standard short-term memory test – which showed that memory recall is better for rehearsed words. Crucially, though, Bem subsequently showed that the number of words that participants recalled in this *first* test could be predicted by a test they took *afterwards*. In this second test, Bem presented participants with half of the original words that they had practised and asked them to sort some into their categories and type out each of the 24 words. The remaining 24 words, which were not seen at this stage, were used as 'no-practice control' words. Bem predicted, and showed, that memory recall in the *first test* was higher for the words that participants would again see in the future, an effect he called 'retroactive facilitation of recall'. Put simply, participants were better at recalling words they saw in the future compared to words they did not see again. His study was accepted in the prestigious *Journal of Personality & Social Psychology*, an outlet that rejects up to 90 per cent of submissions.

But there was a big problem. Precognition is outside of current scientific explanations for human behaviour and conflicts with our understanding of reality. Bem's research was both 'methodologically sound and logically insane' (Engber 2017). This created a bigger problem for psychology – how could Bem have produced such convincing results? Where were the null findings in his nine experiments, which would be expected even when investigating a true phenomenon?

> If one had to choose a single moment that set off the 'replication crisis' in psychology – an event that nudged the discipline into its present and anarchic state, where even textbook findings have been cast in doubt – this might be it: The publication, in early 2011, of Daryl Bem's experiments …
>
> (Engber 2017)

Soon after its publication, many researchers voiced concerns about the methodology and statistical analysis of Bem's research. A mathematical psychologist, Eric-Jan Wagenmakers, recalled how reading Bem's paper made him feel 'physically unwell' (as cited in Engber 2017). Wagenmakers noted that there were many ways in which Bem could have analysed his data, slicing and dicing so that the results would turn up trumps. He couldn't keep quiet, and with a team of collaborators wrote a reply to Bem's paper that made a heartfelt request to the whole of psychology: 'We hope the Bem article will become a signpost for change, writing on the wall: Psychologists must change the way they analyze their data' (Wagenmakers et al. 2011: 431).

The only way to settle this debate was through replication. Could independent teams of researchers find this effect again? The answer to this question was a resounding no. Across seven experiments with over 3000 participants, Galak and colleagues (2012) failed to replicate the results of Bem's experiments, finding an *effect size* of $d = .04$, which was no different from zero. A further three independent research teams also failed to find the same results (Ritchie et al. 2012), but this wasn't the end of their problems – when Ritchie and colleagues submitted their results to the *Journal of Personality & Social Psychology* (the same journal that accepted Bem's research), the journal editor rejected it, stating that they 'do not publish straight replications' (Ritchie, 2020). It became apparent that the field of psychology loved newsworthy findings but did not care about replications that would question the reality of these effects.

Event #3: Stapel's fraudulent fixings

The year 2011 was a bad one for psychology. In the same year that Bem's study raised questions about how researchers analyse and report their results, an academic named Diedrich Stapel would be found guilty of the unthinkable – fraud. Stapel was a research star, publishing over 250 academic articles, book chapters and conference proceedings and winning numerous prizes for research excellence. One of his widely publicized studies showed how disordered, messy environments gave rise to racial discrimination. In this experiment, during a cleaners' strike at a busy train station in the Netherlands, Caucasian participants were invited to complete a questionnaire while sitting in a seat next to five other chairs. The end chair was always occupied by either a Dutch African or Caucasian man. Unbeknownst to participants, Stapel was not interested in their responses to the questionnaires, but instead how far they sat from the African or Caucasian man when the station was either messy or clean. Supporting his hypothesis, Stapel found that the messier the train station, the further away Caucasian participants sat from the African man. In his paper published in the leading journal *Science*, he suggested that policymakers could fight racism and discrimination by cleaning up untidy environments.

But it wasn't the train station that was untidy, it was Stapel's research conduct. A few years later, after being accused of academic misconduct in several of his research studies, Stapel returned to the very same station in the Netherlands to piece together his ground-breaking experiment. But he didn't recognize it. Panic-stricken, he could not find the location that matched the conditions described in his paper. He knew it was over. He knew he had to confess that he had made up the data (Stapel 2014). Overnight, Stapel's career ended, and he went from being a respected professor to an academic con artist. His name would kick the replication crisis into locomotion. But thankfully, as we will see next, academic misconduct is extremely rare. The majority of researchers have a passion for conducting credible research in the pursuit of scientific knowledge (and it is these people who allow us to detect cases such as this one), but others unfortunately get caught up in an academic system which rewards research quantity, and novelty, over quality.

Event #4: Meta-research shines a light on Questionable Research Practices

Meta-research is a field centred on how researchers *do* research. It includes the themes of methods, reporting, reproducibility, evaluation and incentives (how to *do, report, verify, correct and reward science*; Ioannidis et al. 2015). Steered by recent cases of dubious findings (Bem) and outright fraud (Stapel), researchers began to assess something known as '**Questionable Research Practices**' *(QRPs)*. Detailed in Chapter 3, QRPs exploit the grey area of (historic) scientific norms for collecting and analysing data. In a demonstration of this, Simmons et al. (2011) showed how flexibility in data collection, analysis and reporting can allow a researcher to present 'anything as significant'. In the planning stages of this research, Simmons shared ideas with his collaborators about how a researcher might go down the wrong track: they might analyse the data iteratively as it is collected and stop when they reach statistical significance (a practice known as '*optional stopping*'), or they might perform many different *unplanned* tests, trying different variables when one does not yield $p < .05$ ('*p-hacking*'). Furthermore, when researchers come to write up their research, they might change their predictions to match their results ('Hypothesizing After Results are Known'; Kerr, 1998). The possibilities were endless. Simmons and colleagues then put their thoughts to the test, showing through computer simulations and two experiments that it was unacceptably easy to amass evidence for a *false* hypothesis.

But how bad could it be? Surely these practices would only have a small effect on the data? Their findings shocked scientists globally. Simmons et al. found that researchers could almost double their false positive rate (commonly treated as 5 per cent) by engaging in a single QRP, with this elevating to the dizzy heights of more than 60 per cent when multiple QRPs were used. But Simmons et al. weren't finished. To hammer their message home, they showed how using these practices could make the unbelievable appear to be true: that when people listened to the Beatles song 'When I'm Sixty-Four', they were statistically *younger* than they were *before* the song had played. Yes, that's right, just like Bem had predicted time-reversed causality in his studies of precognition, Simmons and colleagues had time-reversed ageing! Their findings stood as a stern lesson to psychologists: chasing statistical significance is disastrous for science.

But how prevalent were these practices? This is precisely what John et al. (2012) aimed to find out in their large-scale survey of 2000 researchers. But here they did something very clever – not only did they ask researchers to report on their own practices, but they also asked them to report how many occasions their colleagues had engaged in QRPs. Surprisingly, given the self-report nature of this survey, the percentage of researchers who admitted to using one or more QRPs was high; over 60 per cent had failed to report all of their dependent measures, more than 50 per cent had engaged in *optional stopping*, and over 40 per cent had selectively reported only experiments that had 'worked'. Unsurprisingly, these researchers also reported that their colleagues had engaged in this much more than they had. Many of the respondents felt that these practices were defensible because they constituted academic norms at the time. Thankfully, as we will find out in Chapter 4, open science aims to improve the credibility of science by shifting this norm so that QRPs are no longer justifiable. Meta-research has opened our eyes to simple decisions that can harm scientific progress.

Event #5: Psychology's crisis of confidence

It's 2012 and the unearthing of a series of unfortunate events influences Pashler and Wagenmakers to declare that psychology is facing a 'crisis of confidence'. In their special issue in the journal *Perspectives on Psychological Science* (*PoPs*), they compiled different viewpoints on a brewing replication crisis and looked for explanations. In response, some scholars argued that claims of a crisis were premature (Stroebe and Strack 2014) and that replication issues were not new (Spellman 2015), while others recommended that replication should be rewarded as a sure and simple way of improving psychological science (Koole and Lakens 2012). The issue also noted some work in progress – a large-scale attempt by the Open Science Collaboration (2012) which would empirically clarify whether psychology was facing a replication crisis. But even with these findings still unknown for the time being, the special issue ended with a positive note that would ripple throughout the scientific community: examples of fraud, QRPs and failed replication attempts allowed psychology to rise and find ways to fix errors, overcome bias and build a literature that people could trust.

Event #6: 'Many Labs' unite

In 2014, the first large-scale replication attempt in psychology was published. In a mammoth collaborative effort known as 'Many Labs', Klein et al. (2014) tested the replicability of 13 classic psychological findings across 12 countries and 6344 participants. These effects were selected based on three criteria: they were relatively short studies, with a simple design, that could easily be conducted online. One of the studies that underwent replication was the 'sunk cost fallacy' – a phenomenon whereby people are more likely to continue doing something when they have already invested time, effort or money in it (Oppenheimer and Monin 2009). For example, imagine that you have tickets to watch your favourite football team, but on the day of the match it starts to pour with rain. Would you be more likely to attend if you had already purchased your ticket? Other examples of selected studies were one investigating the influence of gain versus loss framing on risk-taking (Tversky and Kahneman 1981) and another showing sex differences in implicit attitudes towards mathematics or arts (Nosek et al. 2002).

The findings appeared to be a great success: 77 per cent of the studies (10/13) replicated the original findings! One study assessing the effectiveness of imagined social contact in reducing prejudice (Husnu and Crisp 2010) showed weak support for replicability, with only 4 out of the 36 samples showing a significant effect. The two that did not replicate were priming studies – a technique in which the introduction of one stimulus influences how people respond to another stimulus. In the first, researchers were unable to replicate the finding that subtle exposure to the American flag increases conservatism (Carter et al. 2011), and in the second, priming participants with money did not lead them to express more capitalistic beliefs and behaviours (Caruso et al. 2013).

Psychological findings were highly replicable, hooray! But perhaps not. Some researchers argued that there was a flaw in the Many Labs 1 project (which was even identified by the Many Labs authors themselves): several of these classic studies were already thought to be highly replicable. Strictly speaking, others argued, all this study could tell us was that there were *at least* ten effects in the whole of psychology that could be successfully replicated (Yarkoni 2013).

Event #7: The Open Science Collaboration

Demonstrating that good science takes considerable time, it wasn't until 2015 that the Open Science Collaboration (OSC) published the *Reproducibility Project: Psychology*. Overcoming the limitations of Many Labs 1, their team of over 270 international researchers aimed to replicate 100 *randomly selected* findings from top-tier psychology journals. Moreover, to ensure that the findings would be bulletproof, they spoke to the original study authors to get confirmation on the design, increased their sample size to ensure they had enough *statistical power*, and registered their methods and analysis plans before collecting a single participant to mitigate any researcher bias. Examples of original research questions that were selected for replication included: *Does people's belief that human behaviour is predetermined encourage cheating? Do children blindly follow eye gaze to find hidden objects? Is there a motion 'after-effect' from still photographs depicting motion?* The results would send shockwaves through the field, and land media headlines globally: only 36 per cent of these psychology studies successfully replicated with a p-value below .05. Moreover, social psychology fared particularly badly, with only 25 per cent of effects replicating, compared with 50 per cent from cognitive psychology. To put these findings into context, if the original effects were true, then a minimum replication rate of 89 per cent would have been expected (Field et al. 2019). Even among the studies that did replicate, the *effect sizes* decreased by approximately half compared to the originals. Predictably, these results caused uproar in the scientific community. Were we watching the demise of psychology? Would anyone ever take our field seriously again? But importantly, as we will return to below, there are many explanations for a failed replication, and these can mark the start of a scientific revolution (Kuhn 1962; Redish et al. 2018).

Event #8: 1500 scientists lift the lid on reproducibility

The results of the Open Science Collaboration (2015) struck the field of psychology like a thunderstorm. Well-trusted psychological findings had crumbled overnight, and loud waves rippled through university departments as people discussed which finding was next to break. But despite our discipline being the poster child of failed replications, we were soon to realize that we were not riding the storm alone.

In 2016, Baker surveyed 1500 scientists to investigate concerns about replication and reproducibility across scientific fields. Approximately 90 per cent of respondents from chemistry, medicine, physics and engineering agreed that there was a 'crisis', ranging from significant (52 per cent) to slight (38 per cent). What was more shocking, however, was that while an average of 40 per cent of scientists had struggled to reproduce their own experiments, this increased to over 60 per cent when attempting to reproduce another scientist's findings. Chemistry appeared to fare the worst, with over 85 per cent of researchers experiencing failure to reproduce someone else's results. Sadly, I had no idea of these issues when completing my PhD, but in this article, Professor Marcus Munafò mirrors my own early experiences perfectly: 'I tried to replicate what looked simple from the literature, and wasn't able to', he says. 'Then I had a crisis of confidence, and then I learned that my experience wasn't uncommon' (Baker 2016: 452). As well as outlining the issues, Baker looked at many different reasons for the 'crisis', as well as presenting corrective measures. We will take a deeper look into these in the next chapters, but one thing was clear: the replication crisis had gone mainstream.

Case study: Is the construct of 'ego depletion' too good to be true?

Many classic psychological phenomena are taught in social psychology textbooks without consideration of replication concerns. They are taught as though they are fact, without assessing the flip side of the coin. Here we will take a closer look at the current landscape of one of these: *ego depletion*.

The theory behind ego depletion suggests that willpower is like a muscle – we all have a finite store of energy for self-control and decision-making, and when this is sapped, it is difficult to resist our temptations or make tough decisions. This theory was developed by Baumeister et al. (1998) and put to the test in four experiments. Experiment 1 showed that people who forced themselves to eat radishes instead of yummy chocolates were quicker to quit an impossible quiz compared to those who did not have to exert this self-control. In Experiment 2, this same effect was shown with participants giving up faster on a quiz when they were given the choice to deliver a counter-attitudinal speech, and in Experiment 3 when people were asked to suppress their current emotions. Experiment 4 generalized this effect further, showing that an initial act of self-control could undermine subsequent decision-making. These findings showed seemingly strong support for the notion that self-control draws on limited mental resources that can be 'used up'. Since then, hundreds of studies have investigated ego depletion and this phenomenon has attracted media attention.

But does it replicate? To date, there have been numerous replications which stack up to suggest *possibly not* – there is little evidence to suggest that human willpower works as described (Hagger et al. 2016; Vohs et al. 2021; Xu et al. 2014). In the most recent of these, Vohs and colleagues used a *paradigmatic replication approach*, which selects the experimental procedure based on how well it represents the actual phenomenon, as well as including experts in ego depletion research. Across more than 2000 participants and 20 labs, they found that weakening self-control through two different procedures did not significantly deplete future self-control.

These replication attempts led Michael Inzlicht, an expert in ego depletion research, to turn his back on some of his earlier work. In his attention-grabbing blog titled 'Reckoning with the past', he reflects on these replication attempts:

> As someone who has been doing research for nearly twenty years, I now can't help but wonder if the topics I chose to study are in fact real and robust. Have I been chasing puffs of smoke for all these years? I have spent nearly a decade working on the concept of ego depletion ... I have been rewarded for this work, and I am convinced that the main reason I get any invitations to speak ... is because of this work. The problem is that ego depletion might not even be a thing.
>
> (Inzlicht 2016)

What does 'failure to replicate' mean?

Some people erroneously believe that the results of a replication attempt are definitive – if a study fails to replicate, then the phenomenon must not be real. However, there are many reasons that a replication attempt might not succeed when the original found a significant result, and the truth is that it is really difficult to determine the exact explanation(s).

The first explanation matches people's intuitions – a failed replication might suggest that the original study was a false positive, meaning that it detected evidence for an effect purely by chance. This is particularly likely when we consider that many older studies recruited very small sample sizes and as a result had low **statistical power** to detect reliable effects (i.e. they may have found overestimated, shaky effects; Button et al. 2013; Maxwell 2004). The second explanation is that the replication attempt was a **false negative** (Type II error), meaning that it rejected evidence for an effect when it does exist. This might be because of a critical difference between the original study and the replication attempt that meant the latter did not succeed. It could also be due to methodological confounds, insufficient statistical power or potential moderating variables that make the effect bigger or smaller under certain conditions (Errington et al. 2021a, 2021b; Hagger et al. 2016). Anderson et al., the authors behind the Open Science Collaboration, highlight this beautifully after their intensive efforts to replicate 100 effects in psychology:

> How many of the effects have we established are true? Zero. And how many of the effects have we established are false? Zero. Is this a limitation of the project design? No. It is the reality of doing science, even if it is not appreciated in daily practice. Humans desire certainty, and science infrequently provides it. As much as we might wish it to be otherwise, a single study rarely provides definitive resolution for or against an effect and its explanation.
>
> (Open Science Collaboration 2015: 4716)

Because of these issues, many researchers subscribe to Popper's (2002 [1959]: 64) assertion that 'non-replicable single occurrences are of no significance to science', suggesting that multiple replication studies are required to identify true phenomena (Maxwell et al. 2015). When many replications conclude with similar findings, such as those investigating ego depletion, then research fields can update their beliefs about the body of evidence for a particular theory or phenomenon. They can also decide whether, based on time, effort and resources, it is worth pursuing additional research in that area (Coles et al. 2018).

Are we really in crisis?

In psychology, talks about the replication crisis have been continuing for a decade. But we're also not the only ones, with concerns about replication and reproducibility rippling throughout scientific fields. Worryingly, a recent landmark study showed that only 42 per cent of cancer research studies successfully replicated (Errington et al. 2021a), with reproducibility as low as 10 per cent in this same field (Begley and Ellis 2012; Nosek and Errington 2017). This is a sorry state of affairs when we consider that robust and reliable cancer research is necessary to save people's lives. Furthermore, in a study aiming to replicate structural brain–behaviour correlations in neuroscience, only 1 out of 17 findings were replicated, resulting in a shocking failure rate of 94 per cent (Boekel et al. 2015). With regard to reproducibility, Stodden et al. (2018) found that they were able to retrieve the data from 44 per cent of 204 articles published in the journal *Science* in 2011 and reproduce the findings of only 26 per cent. Similar findings have also been found in economics (~50 per cent; Chang and Li 2022) and preclinical research, with the latter leading to an estimated $28 billion spent on wasteful research (Freedman et al. 2015). However, there are some notable exceptions. Replication attempts in experimental philosophy (~70 per cent; Cova et al. 2021) and economics (61 per cent; Camerer et al. 2016) have reported relatively high success rates compared to other disciplines, but just like the results of Many Labs 1, there are concerns about whether the original studies were selected because they were simply more likely to replicate than others. The larger question is, then, is psychology experiencing a *crisis*, or is this term too strong?

In the early days of psychology's replication efforts, researchers Stroebe and Strack (2014) suggested that the claim of a replication crisis was exaggerated. They argued that exact replications are uninformative because they can never be *exact*, and encouraged the field to focus on conceptual replications. However, this point has been criticized by Simons (2014), who argues that exact replication by multiple laboratories is the only way to verify the robustness of an effect. Simons suggests that if an effect is robust, then any competent researcher (with the right procedures and sample size) should be able to detect it.

Gilbert and colleagues (2016) also argued that the results of the Open Science Collaboration (2015), which suggested a 36 per cent replication success for psychology, might paint a worse picture than reality. One of their arguments was that many of the replication studies recruited different populations than the originals, such as reassessing Americans' attitudes towards African Americans with a sample of Italian participants. They also argued that the replication studies differed procedurally, such as a study that originally gave younger children the difficult task of locating targets on a large screen being repeated with older children given the easier task to locate targets on a smaller screen. They concluded that the OSC project 'allowed considerable infidelities that introduced random error and decreased the replication rate' (Gilbert et al. 2016: 1037). Gilbert and colleagues also argued that the low replication rate could be explained by a lack of endorsement of the replication methodology by the original study authors. Looking closely at the data, they suggested that approved protocols were almost four times more likely to produce successful replications compared to unapproved protocols, implying that 'sign off' by the original authors is important for replication success.

Yet these conclusions were dismissed by Anderson et al. (2016) who, in their reply, suggested that Gilbert and colleagues' assessment was limited by statistical misconceptions and was overly optimistic. Additional Many Labs studies showed that low replication rates are not seemingly explained by variations in samples and settings (Klein et al. 2018b), participant pool quality (Ebersole et al. 2016a) or the approval of the protocols before data collection (Ebersole et al. 2020). One Many Labs study also aimed to test whether involving original authors improves replicability, but rather ironically, they were unable to test this because they couldn't replicate the effect under investigation (Klein et al. 2022). These studies suggest that worries about a 'crisis' are not unfounded and that work is needed to improve psychological science.

While others agree, they also suggest that replication failures are to be expected and are a *normal part of scientific endeavours*. Brian Nosek, the lead researcher on the Open Science Collaboration (2015) project, observes that:

> [replication] is hard. That's for many reasons. Scientists are working on hard problems. They're investigating things where we don't know the answer. So the fact that things go wrong in the research process, meaning we don't get to the right answer right away, is no surprise. That should be expected.
>
> (Nosek, 2015, as cited in Belluz 2015)

This sentiment is mirrored by Redish et al. (2018), who suggest that replication should be a key part of empirical inquiry in any scientific field. They argue that not being able to replicate a study's findings is not necessarily a *failure*, nor does it constitute a *crisis*, but instead opens doors to exploring the underlying factors and limitations of an existing phenomenon. The key to science is that every answer creates new questions (Firestein 2012). This emphasizes that replication failures are part of research – which does not imply that 'bad science' had originally been conducted – and that science needs time to reconcile conflicting findings.

Optimistically, other researchers have renamed the 'replication crisis' the 'credibility' and 'transparency' revolution (Munafò et al. 2017; Fanelli 2018; Vazire 2018). These terms aim to encompass the various ways in which research is improving, such as the recognition that replications are essential and that transparency is key for scientific progress. Within this, there is a renewed focus on self-correction, which is said to be a distinguishing feature of science (Ioannidis 2012; Vazire and Holcombe 2021). As one example of this, a team of researchers published the 'Loss of Confidence' project, in which they admitted that some of their own research studies might not stand up under scrutiny (Rohrer et al. 2021). The great thing about the term 'credibility revolution' is that it documents the recent history of the 'replication crisis' within itself – at first, the idea that psychology was facing a replication crisis was met with worry and apprehension, but more recently this has ushered in fast-paced changes to practice, showcasing how credibility can be achieved. But to ensure long-term improvements, we first need to reflect on *how* and *why* we went wrong. In Chapter 3, I will uncover the many proposed explanations for the replication crisis.

Activity: **The seat of a replicator**

Find your favourite research article from the journal where it was published. See whether there is enough information reported for you to conduct an independent replication.

Ask yourself the following questions:

1   What are the aims or goals of the study?
2   Are there any hypotheses? Are they clearly stated?
3   What is the research design? (e.g. experimental or survey, within-participants, between-participants or mixed?)
4   Who are the sample participants?
5   What is the sample size? Do they provide a rationale for this?
6   What is the independent variable (the *manipulated* variable)?
7   What is the dependent variable (the *measured* variable)?
8   What analyses do they conduct? Is there enough information for you to reproduce these?
9   What is the threshold for reporting statistical significance, or evidence for their hypotheses? Do they provide the *alpha level* (*p*-value) used?
10 Do they report whether they screened or cleaned their data? (e.g. Were there inclusion/exclusion criteria? What did they do with outliers in their data?)
11 What information is missing from the study which might make a replication challenging?
12 Do you expect this study to replicate? Why or why not?

Activity: **Test your knowledge by answering these questions**

1 What is the difference between an 'exact' and 'conceptual' replication?
2 What is the equivalent term for an 'exact' replication?
3 What is the difference between the terms 'replication' and 'reproducibility'?
4 How many studies successfully replicated in Many Labs 1 and how did this differ from the subsequent Reproducibility Project: Psychology?
5 Name three events that sparked the 'replication crisis' in psychology.

3 Causes of the crisis

In Chapter 2, I outlined the recent history of the replication crisis in psychology, considered what 'failures to replicate' mean, and discussed whether the discipline is really in *crisis*. In this chapter, I will take a look below the tip of the iceberg to explore explanations that underpin replication and reproducibility issues in psychology. As you read through, it is important to keep in mind that many of these explanations are intertwined.

Academic incentives reward quantity over quality

To understand the problems associated with research, we first need to look more closely at the people behind it, the *researchers*. Scientists are supposed to be objective, rigorous, rational and dispassionate advocates of knowledge. However, we often forget that they are also human; they have egos, career goals and mortgages to pay (Hardwicke and Wagenmakers 2021). The performance of academics is continuously evaluated; in addition to teaching and administrative duties, they need to publish a certain number of papers in 'top-tier' journals and attract large amounts of funding to build and sustain their research groups (Edwards and Roy 2016). This creates an *academic incentive structure* and leads to a 'publish or perish' mentality, which is a tongue-in-cheek phrase that describes the immense pressure that researchers are under to publish academic outputs and have a successful career (Parsons et al. 2022).

These pressures create a paradox between *what is good for the scientist* and *what is good for science* (Ebersole et al. 2016b). Intrinsic motivations to carry out the best science are overruled by extrinsic motivations centred on quantity over quality: paper after paper, grant after grant. These concerns were first discussed by Meehl (1967) and have surfaced again amid the replication crisis. When asked about the root cause of replication and reproducibility issues in their discipline, Baker (2016) found that over 60 per cent of researchers blamed the pressure to publish. This has led Frith (2020) to encourage the adoption of *slow science*, which suggests that a refocus on quality over quantity would not only be better for science but would also drive down feelings of competition to benefit researchers' well-being.

Bias, bias and more bias

Another issue that affects researchers (and people more generally) is the different *cognitive biases* that change and shape what we see and how we see it

(Munafò et al. 2020). When conducting their research, scientists might fall prey to **confirmation bias**, which is the tendency to search for or interpret information in a manner that supports our prior beliefs (Mahoney 1977). Perhaps instinctively, due to this bias, many will exclaim 'what went wrong?' when the outcome of an experiment does not support their hypotheses, but never ask 'what bias or experimental error could have caused a false positive finding?' (Pusztai et al. 2013). Another cognitive bias is known as **apophenia**, which refers to our natural predisposition to notice patterns in random data and our preference for positive over negative findings. When these two issues collide, they create the larger issue of false positive research – searching for effects that might not exist. Humans can also fall prey to **hindsight bias**, which is the tendency to see an event or finding as predictable only *after* it has occurred (just like Bem's experiments on precognition!). This can lead researchers to write up their research as though they 'knew it all along', painting a seamless but inaccurate picture of the findings (Giner-Sorolla 2012). Thankfully, there are now many ways to protect ourselves from such biases, such as preregistering our research before we collect or analyse the data (see Chapters 4 and 5). But, ironically, these cognitive biases have cascaded to create another bias which is a leading explanation for the replication crisis — **publication bias** deserves a section of its own!

Publication bias

The many biases that researchers fall prey to are reinforced by what kind of research makes it into academic journals. What many students are not taught in higher education is the pathway that a researcher must navigate to get their research published. I used to think that a researcher would submit their article to a journal and hey presto! It would be accepted and published in a couple of weeks. I also thought that it would be equally easy to publish positive and null findings.

The reality is that when a researcher submits their paper to a journal, it undergoes what is known as '*peer review*'. This is an important system that helps to assess the quality of a manuscript before it gets published. Experts in the relevant research field evaluate the manuscript and provide feedback to help journal editors determine whether it should be published in the journal. In doing this, they ask themselves several questions, such as: Is the literature review up to date and accurate? Is the scientific question important? Is the methodology robust and are the measures valid? Are the results reported accurately? And do the conclusions go beyond the data? Many different elements can either be applauded or critiqued, and so they should be – scientific outputs should be rigorous and reliable, and other people should be able to trust that what they read has been appropriately vetted. Figure 3.1 walks us through the peer review process, which has many different stages. But there is a big problem that plagues scientific fields: many peer reviewers and journal editors (the people who ultimately decide whether a paper is accepted or rejected for publication) favour novel studies with positive findings over replication studies or **null findings**.

Figure 3.1 The traditional peer review process for publishing a research article

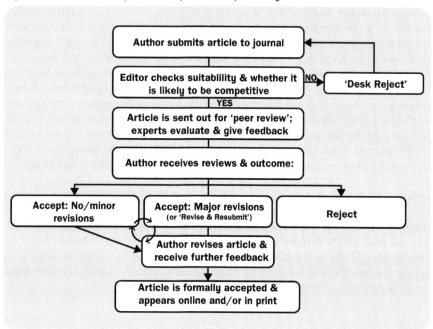

The failure to publish research based on the direction or strength of the findings defines **_publication bias_** (Dickersin 1990). And there may be a rational reason behind it: profitable journals want people to read their contents and get excited about research. If a glossy magazine has the headline 'chocolate cures insomnia' or 'the relationship between chocolate and insomnia (in rats) is complicated', which one are you more likely to read? But the problem is that this can create a literature that is filled with (potentially false) positive findings because journals are more likely to reject non-significant results and researchers may be less likely to submit them (Dickersin 1990; Franco et al. 2014). This creates a _**file drawer problem**_ (Rosenthal 1979), which describes the phenomenon whereby studies with null or inconclusive results are never published and have no findable documentation – they are simply locked away in the rusty file drawer.

This 'prejudice against the null hypothesis' (Greenwald 1975) results in a body of literature that is unrepresentative of the true number of completed studies, 'undead theories' that are popular but have little basis in fact (Ferguson and Heene 2012), and biased effect size estimates in **_meta-analyses_** (Thornton and Lee 2000). Unfortunately, psychology may be among the worst offenders of publication bias. In an analysis of over 2000 articles across scientific disciplines, Fanelli (2010) found that 91.5 per cent of psychology and psychiatry articles presented positive results, which was five times higher than for articles in space science. This has been confirmed in a recent article which found that out of 152 randomly selected psychology articles, 96 per cent reported positive results (Scheel et al. 2021). But *why* is this a problem? Well, as I will explain later in this chapter, the average sample size collected in psychological studies is too low to detect typical effect sizes (Button et al. 2013; Szucs and Ioannidis 2017). This means that psychologists are either *always* testing true hypotheses or something is going awry in the research process. Interestingly, in their mammoth replication study of cancer biology, Errington et al. (2021a) found that original positive findings were only half as likely to replicate compared to null findings.

Publication bias also leads to yet another problem – that of **citation bias**, which is the tendency to disproportionately cite positive compared to null results (de Vries et al. 2018). This is unfortunately common for 'failed' replications; as original articles continue to pick up hundreds of citations as time goes by, their associated replication attempts are left under-recognized and uncited (Hardwicke et al. 2021). Put wonderfully, Heene and Ferguson (2017: 34) argue that psychology has an 'aversion to null results' and this 'distracts from the emphasis on *falsification*, which is necessary for a true science'.

Questionable Research Practices

This immense pressure to publish, influenced by academic incentive structures (get papers!) and publication bias (get lucky!), can lead researchers to overlook the scientific method and work in ways that are detrimental to science. These are known as **Questionable Research Practices (QRPs)**, an umbrella term referring to a range of behaviours that researchers can engage in to – either intentionally or unintentionally – distort their findings (Parsons et al. 2022). There are many different types of QRPs, exemplified in Figure 3.2.

Many of these QRPs centre around the practice of **p-hacking** or **researcher degrees of freedom** (Simmons et al. 2011; Wicherts et al. 2016). These two interchangeable terms describe the many ways in which a researcher can obtain a statistically significant result, which has traditionally been the currency for publication. Figure 3.3 zooms in on different behaviours that are considered *p*-hacking. These include removing outliers *after* looking at their effect on the data, and measuring the same dependent variable in several ways and then only reporting the one that 'worked'. Another form of *p*-hacking is the practice of **optional stopping** (Simmons et al. 2011). This is where a researcher repeatedly analyses their data during ongoing data collection and purposefully decides to stop when the *p*-value reaches a desired threshold (e.g. the magic $p < .05$). This starting-and-stopping creates a 'dance of the *p*-values', meaning that estimates of statistical significance become unreliable (Cumming 2011, 2013). Importantly, optional stopping is not considered a QRP if it is specified in advance and the resulting *p*-value is appropriately corrected (a practice known as 'sequential sampling'; see Lakens 2014). But this is the precise problem with QRPs – they are questionable because they are enacted after getting a feel for the data rather than being guided *a priori* by best practice.

Figure 3.2 A summary of different Questionable Research Practices (QRPs), drawing a line between them and research fraud

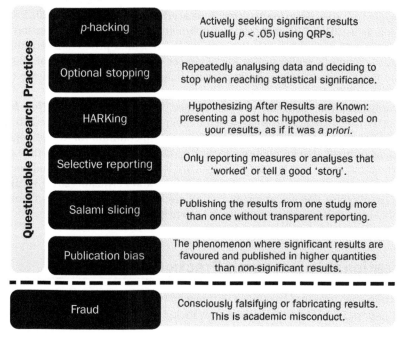

Figure 3.3 Zooming in on *p*-hacking

- Using covariates.
- Excluding outliers.
- Transforming the data.
- Collecting more data (optional stopping).
- Dropping certain conditions/independent variables.
- Measuring the same dependent variable in many different ways.
- Failing to randomly assign participants to experimental conditions.
- Running multiple unplanned analyses ('garden of forking paths').
- Incorrectly reporting or rounding off *p*-values (e.g. $p = .058$ as $p = .05$).
- Analysing sub-sections of the data (e.g. seeing if findings change on demographic variables).
- Using terms such as 'marginally' significant when result is in the expected direction but 'non-significant' when the same result is not in the expected direction.

Note: These are various ways of achieving $p < .05$. Many become a QRP because they are not pre-planned; using covariates or dropping outliers is okay if you have planned this but becomes questionable when this is decided after looking at the data.

Yet another QRP is *Hypothesizing After Results are Known (HARKing)*, which occurs when a researcher changes their experimental hypothesis after looking at the direction of their results (Kerr 1998). Suppose a researcher predicts that watching violent video games increases aggressive tendencies, but when they analyse their data they find the opposite: that watching violent video games decreases aggression. They would commit the QRP of *HARKing* by writing their research as though they had predicted this unexpected result all along (usually citing other studies that found this effect to mask their behaviour!). This practice is problematic because it results in *exploratory* research being presented as *confirmatory*, meaning that researchers who engage in this practice always confirm their hypotheses with their results (Rubin 2017). This can create theories that are hard to eradicate and lead to unreplicable findings (Kerr 1998), which greatly distort meta-analyses (Friese and Frankenbach 2020). Combined, these can lead other researchers into new research endeavours that hit a dead end. In Chapter 2, I explained just how prevalent QRPs are in psychology (John et al. 2012), but there are estimates from other disciplines too. Rubin (2017) conducted a review of meta-research which assessed the prevalence of researcher HARKing and found that, on average, 43 per cent of researchers admitted to having engaged in this QRP. In a sample of biomedical scientists, 63 per cent reported having 'HARKed' once, and 39 per cent admitted to doing so more than once (Tijdink et al. 2016). In a qualitative investigation, Butler et al. (2017) found that common QRPs in business studies were themed around playing with numbers, playing with models and playing with hypotheses. The interviewees provided a range of reasons, such as inadequate statistical training, pressure to publish, and the demands and expectations placed on them by peer reviewers and journal editors. Butler et al. argue that there is an ironic paradox: to live up to the image of being a pure science, researchers may find themselves committing impure actions.

Research has also shown that QRPs are used by some undergraduate students in their research reports. Krishna and Peter (2018) found that students mostly engaged in selective reporting (28.3 per cent), excluding data after looking at the results (15.5 per cent), or using the practice of HARKing (15 per cent). This was predicted by their endorsement of QRPs and their perceived supervisors' attitudes towards these practices. Motivation to write a good dissertation, however, negatively predicted use of QRPs. This suggests that the way students are taught influences their endorsement of such practices. The good news, however, was that these admission rates were relatively low, especially when compared to those of researchers. This is unsurprising given that students do not face the same research pressures that their supervisors do. Consistent with this notion, O'Boyle et al. (2017) showed how ugly initial results in student projects can metamorphose into beautiful ones in the published literature. They assessed the prevalence of QRPs in management research and showed that from dissertation to journal article, the amount of statistically non-significant results decreased while the amount of statistically significant ones increased. Under the current reward system, they suggest that researchers engage in QRPs to better their chances of publication, which is supported by research which suggests that achievement goals predict QRP engagement (Janke et al. 2018).

But why are these practices seen as questionable and not fraud? One reason is that many researchers were not aware of the substantial impact that such practices could have on their data until meta-researchers demonstrated this (see Simmons et al. 2011). Many of these practices were indeed commonplace (John et al. 2012). Because of their history, Sijtsma (2016) therefore suggests that QRPs lie in the middle of an ethical continuum, with responsible research conduct at one end and fraud at the other. In recent times, however, these practices have become greatly frowned upon because people are now aware of their negative impact. You can test your knowledge of QRPs in the activity at the end of this chapter.

Statistically significant p-values

There's a theme running throughout these different explanations – an emphasis on statistical significance. Psychologists commonly use Null Hypothesis Significance Testing (NHST) when analysing quantitative research data. This is a frequentist approach to statistics used to test the probability that an observed effect significantly differs from the null hypothesis of no effect/relationship. Such a conclusion is commonly derived from a statistic known as the **p-value**, which is the probability of the observed, or more extreme, data occurring under the assumption that the null hypothesis is true (Fisher 1934, 1955; see also Lakens 2021). Many of you will have been taught about p-values in your research methods and statistics training and will recognize Fisher's (1934) recommendation that $p < .05$ is commonly used to judge whether an effect is statistically significant or not. The problem is that p-values have become the currency for publication across the social sciences. Publication bias means that many non-significant effects are not accepted for publication, so researchers become hunter-gatherers, searching for $p < .05$ and accumulating research papers based on significant results.

But just because a p-value is statistically significant does not mean that the experimental hypothesis is true. *Lindley's paradox* highlights the arbitrary nature of the $p < .05$ threshold, describing how in very large sample sizes, p-values around the .05 region (e.g. $p = .04$) can actually indicate support for the null hypothesis (Lindley 1957). Moreover, we have seen how researchers can use a range of QRPs to magically arrive at a p-value around .05, which can lead to false positives. This heavy reliance on p-values has led some researchers to argue for statistical reform (Colling and Szűcs 2021; Wagenmakers et al. 2011; Wasserstein et al. 2019). While some journals have banned p-values from their pages altogether (Trafimow and Marks 2014), others have argued that statistical significance should be redefined (Benjamin et al. 2018). For example, Benjamin and colleagues (2018) argue that the bar for claiming statistical significance ($p < .05$) is too low and is a causal factor in studies not replicating.

They suggest that the p-value should be lowered to $p < .005$ for new discoveries. However, these sanctions on p-values have been met with heated debate. Many researchers recommend that p-values *should* be reported appropriately and accompanied by other statistical estimates that provide detailed information about a study, such as *effect sizes* or *confidence intervals* (Cumming et al. 2012; Lakens 2013). Others have also argued that researchers should justify the p-value threshold that they want to use (by weighing up the costs of making a Type I or a Type II error; Lakens et al. 2018a; Maier and Lakens 2022). Another recommendation is to invest in evidence-based education to prevent misinterpretation of p-values and their potential for misuse (Lakens 2021; Peng 2015). Furthermore, as I will detail in Chapter 4, a different type of strategy to tackle the replication crisis is to take the focus away from study results and instead restructure the publication process so that emphasis is placed on the best methods (Chambers and Tzavella 2021).

A history of (too) small sample sizes

Another explanation for the replication crisis is that psychology has historically relied on small sample sizes that allowed researchers to maximize quantity (publishing lots of papers) at the cost of quality (detecting true effects; Higginson and Munafò 2016). Smaldino and McElreath (2016) term this the 'natural selection of bad science', suggesting that powerful incentives actively encourage and reward poor research design. But what is the specific problem with small sample sizes? Against what some may think, just because an effect is significant with a small sample size does not mean that it will still be significant with a larger sample (Simmons et al. 2011). With small sample sizes, researchers may therefore lack the *statistical power* to detect reliable effects. Statistical power is the long-run probability that a statistical test correctly rejects the null hypothesis if the alternative hypothesis is true (Cohen 1988; Parsons et al. 2022). It is usually expressed as a percentage, with a higher percentage corresponding to greater statistical power. Statistical power allows a researcher to balance Type I (false positive) and Type II (false negative) error rates and is usually set to a *minimum* of 80 per cent in psychology. This means that, in the long run, a study will have an 80 per cent chance of detecting an effect if it exists and a 20 per cent chance of this being a false negative.

To work out the statistical power of a study, researchers need to know two of three estimates: the effect size of interest, the significance criterion and the planned sample size. To put it simply, if a researcher has two pieces of this puzzle – they expect to find a 'medium' effect based on previous research (Cohen's d = .50) and set their significance criterion to $p < .05$ – then they will be able to find out what sample size they require. Nevertheless, if you look at many older studies in the psychology literature, you'll see that statistical power is *very* rarely mentioned, if at all (despite it being around since the 1930s; see Descôteaux 2007).

Combined with sheer luck, QRPs and/or publication bias, this means that a lot of older studies in the literature suffer from inflated effect sizes (Button et al.

2013; Szucs and Ioannidis 2017). For example, while meta-analyses estimated a medium-sized effect ($d = .62$) for the construct of ego depletion (Hagger et al. 2010), multiple replication attempts have found effect sizes at least six times smaller ($d = .04-.10$; Dang et al. 2021; Hagger et al. 2016; Vohs et al. 2021). Furthermore, the effect sizes found in the Open Science Collaboration (2015) project were half the size of the original studies. Low statistical power undermines the purpose of scientific research by reducing the chance of detecting a true effect when it exists, as well as reducing the likelihood that a statistically significant result reflects a true effect.

Top tip: On observing a small sample size, you may hear someone critique a study by stating 'it had low statistical power'. Despite intuitions, this is incorrect. Just because a sample size is small doesn't mean that the study lacks statistical power. Instead, it depends on the *effect size of interest*. If a researcher expects a large effect size (e.g. based on previous research and/ or a meta-analysis), then a smaller sample size might actually be sufficiently powered. If a researcher expects a small effect size, then a larger sample size is needed. The point is this – statistical power depends on the significance criterion (e.g. $p < .05$), the effect size of interest and the sample size used for a specific analysis.

Measurement schmeasurement

As well as shaky sample sizes, psychology might also suffer from shaky measurement. To answer scientific questions, researchers are tasked with defining and measuring the construct under investigation. For example, to investigate whether a growth mindset can improve intelligence, a researcher must first define and then measure mindset and intelligence. But measurement is hard and complicated. Intelligence is a latent construct, meaning that unlike a human's height, we cannot see or factually measure it. Instead, psychologists infer intelligence by estimating an individual's IQ, which comprises their answers to lots of questions on an intelligence test, adjusted for their age. How do we know that IQ provides a good proxy for intelligence? Well, we have to assess its **construct validity**, which is defined as whether the measure 'behaves' in a way consistent with theoretical hypotheses (Cronbach and Meehl 1955; Fink 2010). Some researchers have argued that one overlooked explanation of the replication crisis is that our measures have poor construct validity (Lilienfeld and Strother 2020; Loken and Gelman 2017).

Highlighting this issue, Flake et al. (2017) conducted a review of 35 articles in a prestigious journal and revealed that, out of 433 unique measurement scales, 40 per cent had no stated source and only 7 per cent explicitly stated that they had been developed by the authors. Of the remaining 53 per cent of scales that were accompanied by a reference, 19 per cent were adapted in some way compared to the original, meaning that their psychometric properties were unknown. Flake et al. (2017) also found evidence of **Questionable Measurement Practices (QMPs)**, which refers to the nondisclosure of validity when such estimates are found to be unsatisfactory. This led them to conclude that many constructs studied in psychology lack appropriate validation, which can contribute to difficulty in replication.

Other researchers have argued that problems with internal and external validity may contribute to the replication crisis (Fabrigar et al. 2020). *Internal validity* refers to how a study establishes a cause-and-effect relationship between the independent and dependent variables (Cook and Campbell 1979). Fabrigar et al. (2020) suggest that a replication attempt may fail if the original study suffered from a threat to validity that causes a spurious effect (i.e. high internal validity of the replication attempt), or if the replication researchers introduce something that did not exist in the original study (i.e. low internal validity of the replication attempt). *External validity* refers to whether the results of an original study can be generalized to other contexts and/or populations (Cook and Campbell 1979). Again, this could influence replication attempts if, for instance, the replication is conducted on a different population to the original, or if the study materials are translated from a different language and participants do not fully understand what is required of them.

Fabrigar et al. (2020) use an example of the facial feedback effect to demonstrate how external validity can influence replication outcomes. The facial feedback hypothesis proposes that subjective experiences of emotions can be directly influenced by an individual's facial expression. In the original study, Strack et al. (1988) asked participants to hold a pen in their mouth in a way that activated the muscles involved in either smiling or pouting: the 'pen-in-mouth task'. Participants were then asked to rate a series of cartoons based on their perceived humour. The findings indicated that participants reported feeling more amused by the cartoons when smiling compared to pouting. In a large-scale replication, Wagenmakers et al. (2016) found no evidence of this facial feedback effect, but Strack (2016) presented numerous problems pointing towards threats to external validity. One of these was that, unlike the original study, participants in the replication were video recorded to ensure that they pulled the correct facial expression, and Strack argued that this may have confounded the study by influencing participant self-consciousness. Two additional studies were conducted to see if this explanation held up under scrutiny; one found evidence for the facial feedback effect when there was no video camera present (Marsh et al. 2019) and the other found that the effect diminished when participants were recorded (Noah et al. 2018). Furthermore, a recent adversarial collaboration (where teams of authors with opposing views work together) calls into question the pen-in-mouth task altogether: while they found that emotion could be amplified by facial mimicry or a voluntary facial action task, the pen-in-mouth task was inconclusive (Coles et al. 2022). This may be because this task cannot reliably produce prototypical emotional facial expressions.

To summarize these issues succinctly, Flake and Fried (2020) refer to them as 'measurement schmeasurement', which describes the lack of consideration for measurement validity in psychological science. If a study's measures are not valid, then it follows that the findings and conclusions drawn from them cannot be either. When these studies are replicated, they may be destined to fail before they even begin.

Favouring novelty over replication

The late nineteenth century marks the birth of experimental psychology, with Wilhelm Wundt setting up the first laboratory dedicated to psychological research in 1879. So why then, after over one hundred years, has psychology now found itself in a replication crisis? The answer: replication studies have not been favoured or rewarded in the social sciences.

In the present publishing culture, the emphasis on novel and positive results means that replications and negative results are a rarity (Makel et al. 2012; Mueller-Langer et al. 2019). Antonakis (2017) suggests that science suffers from 'significosis' – a disproportionate focus on significant findings – and 'neophilia' – an extreme emphasis on novelty. Indeed, many argue that the incentive structure of academia actively discourages replications in the social sciences (Higginson and Munafò 2016; Romero 2017). This insight is not new; Sterling (1959) expressed concern that researchers could repeatedly test a hypothesis in many different experiments until eventually, by chance, they ran into a significant effect. Across laboratories, if these 'lucky' experiments were then published but not replicated, then a whole field could stand on a shocking number of false claims. Tukey (1969: p. 84) supported this point stating that 'Confirmation comes from repetition. Any attempt to avoid this statement leads to failure and more probably to destruction.' But such concerns were not listened to. In 2012, Makel et al. demonstrated that out of 500 articles selected from top-tier journals, only 1.07 per cent were replications. In a follow-up study, Makel and Plucker (2014) assessed 100 education journals and found that only 0.13 per cent were replications. Interestingly, they also found that in both psychology and education research, the majority of replications tended to be 'successful', suggesting that publication bias pervades.

The focus on novelty over replication can also be seen in student research projects, such as the final year dissertation (or thesis; see Button et al. 2016, 2020). In the UK, for example, a psychology student is expected to have 'completed a series of practical reports, culminating in an empirical project reporting on a substantial piece of research' (British Psychological Society 2019: 13). However, such 'substantial' projects are usually undertaken alone, without research funding and under very strict time constraints. In one single university, this can result in hundreds of individually supervised projects that suffer from the same problems seen in the wider literature: underpowered, novel studies that can yield a high rate of false positives (Button et al. 2020). If these are then selectively published, students are rewarded for being lucky rather than right. Equally, many null findings might never make it out of the file drawer (Rosenthal 1979). In Chapter 4, I will show you many new and exciting initiatives that aim to combat these problems, such as the Collaborative Replications and Education Project (CREP; Wagge et al. 2019a), which encourages students to conduct replications as part of their degree, and the consortium approach to the empirical dissertation (Button et al. 2016, 2020).

Science has not been self-correcting

An additional hallmark of the scientific process is self-correction (Merton 1973). However, tied up in academic incentives and concerned with reputational costs, scientists appear to be worried about correcting their mistakes (Bishop 2018; Rohrer 2021). Furthermore, under the pressure of moving on to their next project or grant application, the time needed to continuously evaluate and correct past work becomes a barrier to its implementation (Rohrer 2021). Of the many explanations for the replication crisis, the idea that science is *not* self-correcting is one of them.

As an example, let's look at the ***Registered Replication Report*** of Srull and Wyer (1979) by McCarthy et al. (2018). In the original study, Srull and Wyer demonstrated that priming participants with aggression-related stimuli caused them to interpret a random person's ambiguous behaviour as more hostile. But although the replication attempt went in the same direction as the original, the effect size was considered negligible ($d = .06$). One potential reason for this was that some of the statistics in the original study may have been incorrectly reported (see McCarthy et al. 2018). Nevertheless, this error has still not been confirmed or corrected in the 1979 article. Another example comes from van der Zee et al. (2017), who describe how they experienced 'statistical heartburn' in attempting to reanalyse the data of four articles from the Cornell Food Lab. In a shocking tale of irreproducibility, they identified over 150 inconsistencies in data reporting. Furthermore, Griggs and Whitehead (2014, 2015) discuss several inaccuracies that persist across common psychology textbooks, including errors in the coverage of the Milgram studies and the Stanford prison experiment.

Elizabeth Bik, a microbiologist, reveals that these issues are not specific to psychology. In her commendable work, Bik has identified hundreds of manipulated images in scientific publications. Image manipulation in scientific articles has become an emerging type of misconduct because it is used to make findings look more impressive, or even cover up suspicious data. Highlighting this issue, Bik et al. (2018) analysed 960 papers in *Molecular and Cellular Biology* and found that 59 (6.1 per cent) contained duplicated images. This led to five papers being retracted (where an article is withdrawn from a journal, and marked as a retraction), and 41 corrections. While this may be a sign that science can be self-correcting, it is notable that this job is done primarily by other researchers as voluntary labour; perhaps, then, science is 'other-correcting'.

Demonstrating further that science might not be as self-correcting as we would hope, many 'error detection' researchers have been the target of negative comments and trolling on social media. This suggests that such work makes researchers feel uncomfortable, but Vazire (2020) argues that this discomfort is healthy. Rather than publication marking the 'end' of a particular project, researchers have an ethical responsibility to minimize errors and always be on the lookout for them. From this perspective, Hoekstra and Vazire (2021) make a case for intellectual humility in science, whereby researchers 'own' the limitations of their work indefinitely. They suggest that corrections should be encouraged, and when warranted, articles should be retracted or 'loss of confidence' statements should be published (e.g. Rohrer et al. 2021).

But let's now turn this section on its head – arguably, the replication crisis itself shows that science *is* self-correcting. The replication crisis is a sign that science is working, and the issues we have unearthed are moving us forward. Some researchers have used their mistakes to teach others about the importance of self-correction and to encourage the checking of data, code and analysis (Poldrack 2013). Bishop (2018) suggests that with the new focus on transparency and rigour, we will find that *everyone* is fallible.

Closed science

One of the major barriers to replication and reproducibility is the lack of transparency and detail in previous studies. Think back to Chapter 2 where I introduced you to the stereotypical scientist – he conducted research in a private laboratory under a big sign that said 'KEEP OUT!'. Researchers have approached scientific investigation as though it were a secret recipe, but as a consequence, closed science makes it tricky, if not impossible, for other labs to recreate studies and retest analyses (Wiggins and Christopherson 2019). Figure 3.4 summarizes the behaviours I have highlighted so far.

Figure 3.4 An example of research practices under a system of 'closed' science

Researcher conducts an experiment...
Doesn't declare hypotheses in advance
Doesn't state all of the measures used

Collects the data...
Uses a variety of analysis techniques
Seeks p< .05

Writes the article...
Creates a story ('hype/spin')
'Hypothesizes After Results are Known' ('HARKing')

Submits to a journal...
Never shows data to anyone
Doesn't submit null results

The first problem is the under-reporting of methodological details in published articles (Flake and Fried 2020; Errington et al. 2021a, 2021b). Transparency is essential because the research process includes hundreds of decisions, and unless these are explained clearly, no one will know what the researcher did. In addition to Flake et al. (2017), who found that many articles did not state the source of their measurement scales, similar issues have been found in the reporting of systematic reviews and meta-analyses (Campbell et al. 2019; López-Nicolás et al. 2022) and experimental studies (A. Jones et al. 2021; Pennington et al. 2021) that expand psychology (Errington et al. 2021b). For example, research has estimated that between only 1 and 14 per cent of research articles share their materials (Adewumi et al. 2021; Hardwicke et al. 2022), and in my research field of addiction science, just 38 per cent of articles explained where they sourced experimental task stimuli (Pennington et al. 2021). Thankfully a move to **open materials** (see Chapter 5) can help to mitigate this problem, but it stands frozen in time for older articles whose materials remain unavailable.

These problems also generalize to the availability of data and the reporting of analyses. There are many analytical decisions that a researcher makes during the data analysis stage, such as whether and how to look at data outliers, what to do if the data do not meet certain statistical assumptions, or how to correct for multiple analyses. All of these decisions constitute a normal part of the research process rather than representing immoral intent. However, as outlined in the section on QRPs, if researchers do not transparently report their analysis plan, or they make decisions after viewing the data that no one else knows about, then their results can differ dramatically (and everyone else has a tough time reproducing them). These unplanned decisions are generally referred to as the **garden of forking paths** (Gelman and Loken 2014), and Figure 3.5 provides an example of this.

This is further exemplified by an impressive initiative known as 'Many Analysts', which aims to teach other researchers how different researcher decisions can vastly impact study findings (e.g. Botvinik-Nezer et al. 2020; Silberzahn et al. 2018). Silberzahn and colleagues (2018) crowdsourced 29 teams including 61 analysts, presenting them with a research question and a data set – are soccer referees more likely to give more red cards to players with dark-toned or light-toned skin? The analysts were simply instructed to analyse the data in any way that could answer this question. Twenty teams (69 per cent) found a significant positive effect, while the remaining nine teams (31 per cent) observed a non-significant effect. Overall, *none of the teams* used the same analysis or the same variables. You can hopefully now see that closed science poses a huge issue for both replication and reproducibility.

But there's a solution! Surely if data was made openly available, then others could simply check it and rerun those analyses? According to the ethical principles that underpin psychological research, data *should* be shared so that other researchers can verify the findings (APA 2002). Nevertheless, compliance with this ethical code is far from commonplace. Wicherts et al. (2006) discuss how they hit many dead ends when trying to retrieve 249 data sets from empirical articles published in APA journals, stating that: 'unfortunately, 6 months later, after writing 400 e-mails and … signed assurances not to share data with

Figure 3.5 An example of the garden of forking paths. Starting with a research question, a researcher can make many different methodological and analytical decisions that impact the research findings. Making such decisions based on the results can lead to false positives

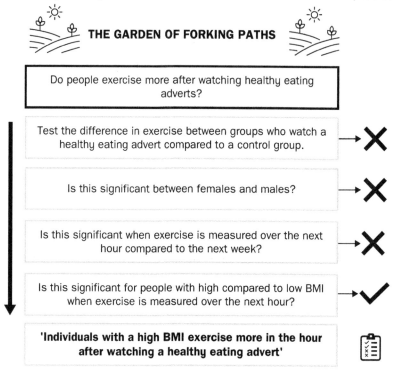

others, we ended up with a meager 38 positive reactions and the actual data sets from 64 studies (25.7%). This means that 73% of authors did not share their data' (p. 727).

Open data still seems to be a sticking point despite technical developments that have greatly facilitated data sharing; Vanpaemel et al. (2015) could only obtain 38 per cent of datasets from 394 papers published in APA journals in 2012. But again, this is not just an issue in psychology; Chang and Li (2015) report that approximately half of the failed reproducibility attempts in economics were caused by authors not submitting the data files, with similar findings in genetics (Ioannidis et al. 2009). Furthermore, in their attempts to replicate cancer research, Errington et al. (2021b) ran into many problems accessing data, which meant that their original plan to replicate 193 experiments from 53 papers turned into replicating 50 experiments from 23 papers. Although there may be, at times, valid reasons not to share data, such as ethical considerations (e.g. ensuring participant anonymity), which are a particular concern in qualitative research (Prosser et al. 2022), these should always be transparently stated so that others simply know. Miyakwa (2020) goes so far as to say, 'no raw data, no science'.

***Activity*: Spot the Questionable Research Practices (QRPs)**

Read the following hypothetical examples and identify:

1 What is the QRP?
2 Why is it problematic?
3 How can this be overcome? (Hint, see Chapter 5)

Example 1: Angelo wants to examine the influence of caffeine on attention. He decides to carry out multiple studies addressing this research question. In the first study, 40 participants complete an attention task, drink a cup of coffee containing 200 mg of caffeine, and then complete the attention task for the second time. In the second study, 50 participants drink 400 mg of caffeine before completing the attention task. In a third study, participants are randomly assigned to one of three groups: one group drink a cup of water (control), one group drink 200 mg of caffeine, and the final group drink 400 mg of caffeine before completing the attention task.

Angelo analyses the results of his studies and finds that both Experiment 1 and 2 demonstrate that caffeine significantly impacts attentional resources. However, Experiment 3 shows no significant effect. He writes his study up for publication in a journal, and reports both Experiment 1 and 2, but decides not to report Experiment 3. The article is published after peer review and goes on to be cited over 500 times within the next two years. Angelo presents his findings at conferences and engages in public talks about the influence of caffeine on attention.

Example 2: Billie conducts a study on the influence of violent video games on self-reported aggression. She assigns participants to either a 'violent video game' condition (Grant Theft Auto) or a 'non-violent video game' condition (Animal Crossing). She then measures perceived mood and aggressive tendencies using a variety of measures. When writing up the findings, she finds that the influence of violent video games on perceived mood is not significant. However, the impact of violent video games on aggressive tendencies is. Billie writes up the findings focusing on aggressive tendencies, and reports that participants who played Grand Theft Auto reported significantly higher aggressive tendencies compared to those who played Animal Crossing. Her article 'Violent video games cause aggressive tendencies' attracts a lot of attention from the press and the general public.

Example 3: Dr Jenks runs an experiment to investigate the influence of rewards on children's eating behaviour. She predicts that children eat more vegetables when they are rewarded with stickers after each meal, compared to when they are not rewarded with stickers. She recruits 60 parent–child pairs and asks parents to count how many vegetables their children eat after receiving stickers for a previous meal. After four weeks, Dr Jenks analyses the findings. Contrary to her prediction, children eat *fewer* vegetables when they have previously been rewarded with a sticker compared to when they receive no reward. This makes sense to Dr Jenks; previous research has shown that the reward salience of the stickers diminishes over time! She writes up the findings and states that she predicted children would eat *fewer* vegetables when they receive rewards, and then confirms this hypothesis with her findings.

In this chapter, I have explored many different causes for the replication crisis in psychology, many of which are born out of dysfunctional academic incentives. At this point you may be thinking, how can psychology reinstate its credibility? Is this discipline *really* built on quicksand? You'll be glad to hear that it's now time for some optimism! In Chapter 4, I will show you how psychology is becoming the front-runner for reflection, self-correction, credibility and transparency in research. A movement of 'open science' has ushered in fast-paced changes in the way that research is conducted, evaluated and rewarded. Personally, this has reinvigorated my early love for psychology and got me excited for its future! It's time to close this door on closed science and welcome you through the door of *open science*.

4 Crisis averted! Open science reform

In Chapter 3, I discussed the interlocking causes that underpin the replication crisis in psychology. I looked closely at how cognitive biases influence what research is published, how current academic incentives reward research quantity over quality, and how researchers under pressure may be driven to engage in questionable research or measurement practices. After diving into problems that arise when we predominantly focus on statistical significance, I then considered the after-effects in a field that has prioritized novelty over replication, allowed mistakes to go uncorrected and permitted science to be conducted behind closed doors. You'll be pleased to know that this chapter has a more positive outlook! It will teach you about the *open science* reform, which has arguably turned the replication crisis into psychology's credibility revolution.

Open science is an umbrella term reflecting the idea that knowledge of all kinds should be openly accessible, transparent, rigorous, reproducible and replicable (Crüwell et al. 2019; Kathawalla et al. 2021). It also includes scrutinizing whose voices are represented in science, to confront all sources of bias (Ledgerwood et al. 2022; Murphy et al. 2020; Pownall et al. 2021; Whitaker and Guest 2020). It's important to remember that the term *open science* is used interchangeably with *open research* to encompass all research disciplines, and *open scholarship* to include its teaching and pedagogy (Parsons et al. 2022). The pursuit of open science is facilitated by several different practices, as shown in Figure 4.1. Some of these practices focus on making the existing research process more transparent, some try to change the way that research is done, and some do both. Nonetheless, they all have the same overarching goal: to improve science.

In this chapter, I will outline the proposed benefits of these open science practices, mapping these onto the explanations of the replication crisis presented in Chapter 3. I will also discuss some emerging empirical evidence for how these are faring in psychological science. With this in mind, it's important to remember that more evidence, both for and against these practices, will emerge in the future. This is exciting because you can use this book as the basis for your knowledge of open science and then build it up as additional empirical work is published.

Preprints

Researchers want their work to be read and used by others, and one avenue to achieve this is publishing in academic journals. A big problem, however, is that many journal articles are stuck behind a 'paywall', meaning that other researchers

Figure 4.1 Different practices under the umbrella of open science

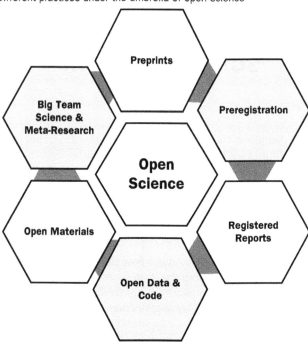

and the general public can only read the article if they are affiliated with an institution that funds a licence, or they pay to read it themselves. Another way of publishing is *open access* – which refers to the unrestricted public availability of research products (Crüwell et al. 2019). Authors can pay a lump sum to a journal, known as an 'Article Processing Charge' (APC), which allows other people to access the work for free. But herein lies another problem: researchers need to have money to pay for open access publishing, but many do not have grant income or other institutional funding to cover these costs. You may need to read this paragraph again for it to make (some kind of) sense – researchers conduct research, and then typically hand over the copyright of their article to a journal unless they pay a fee to make it open access. When I explain this publishing system to my parents, they look at me confused and say 'What? You have to pay to publish your work so others can read it? And if you don't, people have to pay to access it?' The answer, historically, has been yes.

Nosek and Bar-Anan (2012) argue that making research open access can contribute to scientific utopia, and many research funders now agree with this sentiment too. However, there is a practice that can bypass the payment of such open access licences altogether, allowing researchers to share their work publicly. The term *preprint* refers to a scientific document made available freely and legally outside of traditional publishers, through an online internet repository (Moshontz et al. 2021). Importantly, the term *preprint* describes an author's unpublished work that hasn't yet undergone peer review, whereas the term *postprint* refers to the final version of this work that will soon be published in an academic outlet. Interestingly, many preprint repositories have been around for decades (Cobb 2017), but only recently have they been adopted in psychology. For example, the preprint server named 'arXiv' celebrated its thirtieth birthday in 2021 and currently hosts over 2 million preprints in physics, mathematics and computer sciences. In comparison, the psychology-dedicated server 'PsyArXiv' was founded in 2016 by the Center for Open Science and the Society for Improving Psychological Science (Abdill and Blekman 2019; Moshontz et al. 2021). In recent years, more preprint repositories have been born, such as those for the health sciences (medRxiv) and education research (EdArXiv).

A particular benefit of preprints is that they ensure public access to research, supporting the notion that science is collectively owned, and usually funded, by the general public (Moshontz et al. 2021). Preprints also hold many benefits for researchers themselves, such as allowing them to gain helpful feedback pre-publication, and to disseminate their research more quickly (Tennant et al. 2016), and it is for these reasons that many journals now allow researchers to preprint their article before submission. Recall the peer review process that I explained in Chapter 3? Well, the time elapsed between article submission and publication can be *years*: Nosek and Bar-Anan (2012) provide a case study where their article took 677 days to appear in print! By the time an article sees the light of day, there may have been numerous additional studies published, meaning that a lot of the cited literature will already be outdated. Because preprints are visible in the early days, and their metrics can be merged with the final published article, they can increase the number of citations gained by up to 40 per cent (Fu and Hughey 2019). And this offers yet another advantage, aiding collaboration between researchers who can comment on each other's work or see overlaps with their own interests.

But these are mainly selfish reasons to share preprints. The crucial question is how do preprints help the replication crisis? By making research papers available before publication, other readers can evaluate the claims and spot any errors. This can aid self-correction because these errors are identified before it's too late and the research enters the published literature (and researchers can simply update their preprint). Furthermore, preprints can fight *publication bias* by allowing researchers to share outputs that would otherwise be relegated to their file drawer. This can increase the reliability of meta-analyses that pool data across studies, and also offer useful information to researchers who want to pursue a new line of research. Finally, preprints can increase *transparency* as many repositories have inbuilt version control so that readers can see any changes to the original document, which is particularly beneficial after the article has undergone several rounds of peer review (Bourne et al. 2017). Arguably, study preprints might also aid *reproducibility*. This is because many researchers argue that a barrier to methodological and analytical transparency is the strict word count guidelines that journals often impose. Making the internet the primary vehicle for scientific communication removes the printing and shipping costs associated with academic journals, and freely available preprint servers allow authors to submit as many documents as they wish. While alone preprints may not be a panacea, alongside the adoption of many other open science practices, they can provide a solution to closed science.

Preregistration

In standard journal articles, it's very difficult to tease apart whether a researcher's hypotheses were conceived before or after knowing the results, and whether the analyses are thus confirmatory or exploratory (Nosek et al. 2018; Wagenmakers et al. 2012). We therefore need a practice that can transparently distinguish *prediction* from *postdiction* (Nosek et al. 2018). One such practice is study **preregistration**, which refers to the initiation of a time-stamped, uneditable document of the research questions, hypotheses, methods and analysis plans before data collection and/or analysis (Nosek et al. 2018; van 't Veer and Giner-Sorolla 2016). There are several different preregistration registries that each host their own templates, including AsPredicted (www.aspredicted. org), the Open Science Framework (www.osf.io) and clinicaltrials.gov (www. clinicaltrials.gov; see Nosek et al. 2019). Each template provides a structured workflow that asks researchers to answer several questions, ranging from listing each of their hypotheses to justifying the sample and analysis plans. Importantly, researchers are asked to clearly distinguish between confirmatory and exploratory analyses – both are valued by preregistration (Simmons et al. 2020a). Preregistration can be used for all kinds of research methodologies including quantitative and qualitative designs, and those that utilize **secondary data** (e.g. Bosnjak et al. 2022; Haven and van Grootel 2019; van den Akker et al. 2021a).

The first registry — clinicaltrials.gov — was implemented in 2000 after the US Congress passed a law mandating that all experimental drug trials should be accessible to the general public (US Food and Drug Administration Act, 1997, 2007). Shortly after, in 2005, many leading medical journals began requiring trial registration as a prerequisite for publication (Zarin et al. 2017; Zou et al. 2018). The preregistration of clinical trials is proposed to have numerous benefits, such as meeting ethical obligations to participants, enhancing patient access to enrolment in clinical trials and, importantly, preventing the duplication of trials for knowingly unsafe or ineffective treatments. Furthermore, this practice allows other researchers to evaluate research integrity by assessing whether researchers adhere to their preregistration (Zarin and Keselman 2007).

Preregistration in psychology came a lot later, however. The Center for Open Science was founded in 2013 with a mission to increase openness, integrity and reproducibility of research, and they developed the Open Science Framework (OSF, www.osf.io; Foster and Deardorff 2017) — an open-source platform to facilitate the transparency of research. The OSF hosts many different preregistration templates that guide researchers through the process and then, after initiation, safely stores a time-stamped copy. Another platform, 'AsPredicted', was created by the University of Pennsylvania's Wharton Credibility Lab in 2015 (Simmons et al. 2018, 2020a) and asks researchers eight questions regarding their planned research. Given that this practice is quite new, you might think that uptake would be slow (after all, changing human behaviour is hard). In reality, the number of initiated preregistrations is growing exponentially! While there were only 38 preregistrations on OSF in 2012 (Nosek and Lindsay 2018), this has now skyrocketed to over 100,000 as of 2022 (https://osf. io/registries/discover). Similarly, over 1200 new studies are preregistered on AsPredicted every month and, to date, over 80,000 (as of today) preregistrations have been uploaded from over 2100 institutions (Simmons et al. 2020a; https://credlab.wharton.upenn.edu/).

While some people are sceptical of preregistration (see Pham and Oh 2021a, 2021b), many of these concerns are unfounded (see Simmons et al. 2020a, 2020b). Instead, preregistration is proposed to protect researchers against their *cognitive biases* by getting them to transparently state their plans before the data is collected, or in the case of **secondary data** before the analyses have been conducted (Hardwicke and Wagenmakers 2021; Munafò et al. 2017). This helps restrain *researcher degrees of freedom* and mitigate *QRPs* such as selective reporting and *p*-hacking, or make them more detectable (Nosek et al. 2018; O'Connor 2021; Simmons et al. 2020a, 2020b). Furthermore, preregistration can help prevent *publication bias* by making research more discoverable (Munafò et al. 2017; Nosek et al. 2018, 2019), and the added transparency can increase the credibility of scientific research (Hardwicke and Wagenmakers 2021). From a philosophy of science perspective, preregistration allows others to evaluate whether a proposed hypothesis can be falsified (known as 'the severity of a test'; Lakens 2019). However, it's important to note that preregistration is not a cure-all practice: while it can increase transparency, it doesn't magically fix a study based on bad theory or design.

But all of these are proposals of what preregistration *should* do. This begs the question: what does the empirical data on preregistration tell us so far? I have some great news! A recent study by van den Akker and colleagues (2021b) provides some preliminary data to suggest that the percentage of positive results reported from preregistered studies is around 65 per cent. This is in blunt contrast to the estimate of over 90 per cent in the standard (non-preregistered) literature (Fanelli 2010; Scheel et al. 2021; Sterling 1959). Furthermore, Kaplan and Irvin (2015) showed that before clinical trial registration was introduced in 2000, 57 per cent of studies reported that the intervention was effective, but this dropped to only 8 per cent after registration was implemented. This suggests that preregistration may work as a strategy to reduce publication bias and effectively mitigate QRPs. Furthermore, where researchers provide detailed information in their preregistration, this aligns well with the corresponding publication (van den Akker et al. 2021b).

Unfortunately, though, research also suggests that many preregistrations lack detail and specificity (Bakker et al. 2020; TARG Meta-Research Group and

Collaborators 2021), meaning that it's sometimes difficult to even evaluate their effectiveness. In addition, where discrepancies and changes do arise between pre-registrations and final publications, many of these are undisclosed (Claesen et al. 2021; Heirene et al. 2021; TARG Meta-Research Group and Collaborators 2022). There are many potential reasons for these issues, such as misaligned incentives for preregistration or a lack of sufficient training. On the flip side, many discrepancies might arise due to the difficult process of conducting research – for example, you might notice a simple mistake in your preregistration or learn something new that invalidates your original plans, and with transparent disclosure this is perfectly okay. However, without a standardized way of reporting discrepancies (Goldacre et al. 2019), and with many peer reviewers admitting that they don't check preregistrations (Mathieu et al. 2013), this can reintroduce bias into the research process. Thankfully, the Open Science Framework recognized this problem and have implemented a new 'update' feature to preregistrations initiated on their platform, and further efforts are under way to develop tools that make it easier to report preregistration-publication discrepancies and to facilitate their peer review (TARG Meta-Research Group and Collaborators 2022). But one publishing format that has foreseen many of these problems and already provides the solutions is that of Registered Reports.

Registered Reports

Let's put it bluntly – tomorrow, you are diagnosed with a life-threatening illness. You want to know what treatment will help you survive, so you start looking through the published literature. You see that two drugs are highly effective with low side effects. You go to your doctors and tell them you've made the decision to take one of these drugs. Now let's assume that publication bias is rife – the positive effects of the drug are published in abundance, but the negative or null results are either not submitted or rejected by editors. Researchers use QRPs because they are worried that, if they don't publish, they won't hit their performance evaluations and keep their jobs. Should science be based on the truth or the saleability of a finding? Your life is literally in their hands! For some, this is not a hypothetical scenario: Nosek (2017) tells a heart-breaking personal story about why open science means so much to him.

We therefore need a strategy that can ensure research is published regardless of the results – a strategy that favours methodological rigour and detail more than flashy findings. Thankfully, Registered Reports offer a different way of conducting research that moves peer review to a much earlier stage in the research process and, by doing so, allows researchers to embed study preregistration within the written article itself. Let's pull this apart a little bit more. In the traditional publishing model, after a researcher has conducted their study, they write up a research article that typically comprises an introduction, method, results and discussion. If the researcher has preregistered their study, they will note this in their methods section and provide a direct link to their preregistration, which is hosted on a verified online platform. They then submit

Figure 4.2 The Registered Report publishing model. Peer review occurs at two stages known as Stage 1 and Stage 2. Preregistration occurs naturally within the submission of a Stage 1 article

this to a journal and, based on the peer reviews, the journal editor either accepts or rejects the study: if there are methodological flaws, then tough, it's too late. Registered Reports, on the other hand, split this peer review process into two stages, as shown in Figure 4.2.

At Stage 1, researchers follow the Registered Reports guidance and submit a proposal that includes an introduction, method and analysis plan (imagine a traditional research article cut in half). They then benefit from peer review in this planning stage, with reviewers providing helpful feedback to improve the study before data collection and/or analysis begins. Following detailed peer review, and after implementing any revisions, researchers can then be offered something called 'in principle acceptance' (IPA), which is where a journal accepts the Stage 1 article and commits to publishing the research *regardless of the results*. As part of this process, the study also becomes preregistered automatically. The researchers then collect their data or, in the case of secondary data, conduct their analyses and submit a Stage 2 manuscript, which knits the results and discussion section to the original proposal. The reviewers then double-check that the authors have stuck to their plans (or that any deviations were approved and are transparently reported) and that the results have been interpreted appropriately (no *hype* or *spin*), before offering final acceptance (Chambers and Tzavella 2021). Importantly, at this point, the reviewers are not allowed to voice any concerns about any part of the Stage 1 proposal, and they are not allowed to get upset about the results! Registered Reports therefore simply work on the premise that to foster replicability and reproducibility, we need to focus on the research process itself and not the outcomes (Grand et al. 2018). Rather than trying to achieve statistical significance, researchers instead focus their efforts on designing important and methodologically sound research (Rosenthal 1966; Walster and Cleary 1970).

> There is a cardinal rule in experimental design that any decision regarding the treatment of data must be made prior to an inspection of the data. If this rule is extended to publication decisions, it follows that when an article is submitted to a journal for review, the data and the results should be withheld. This would insure that the decision to publish, or not to publish, would be unrelated to the outcome of the research.
>
> (Walster and Cleary 1970: 17)

I want you to look back at those last references again and note the dates. 1966? 1970? You might think I have made a mistake. In fact, you may be astonished to hear that Registered Reports are not a brand-new idea! Rosenthal (1966) originally proposed the idea of Registered Reports suggesting that a system was needed for evaluating research solely based on the procedures employed. In 1976, this publishing model was even formalized by parapsychologist Martin Johnson in the *European Journal of Parapsychology*, but it was then retired in 1992 and remained unknown to the wider scientific community (Chambers and Tzavella 2021; Wiseman et al. 2019). Amid rumbles of the replication crisis in psychology, the idea was resurrected in 2012, being proposed simultaneously by the editors of the journals *Cortex* (Chambers 2013) and *Perspectives on Psychological Science* (Eich 2013). It was then formally offered to authors in 2013 by those journals, along with another journal, *Social Psychology* (Nosek and Lakens 2014). But this time, it appears that Registered Reports are here to stay, with over 300 journals now offering them. Furthermore, an initiative named *Peer Community In Registered Reports* (PCI RR; https://rr.peercommunityin.org/) was launched in April 2021 to facilitate the peer review of Registered Report *preprints* (Chambers and Tzavella 2021; Pennington and Heim 2022). This removes the need for journals altogether to envisage a brand new way of publishing. PCI RR offers a multitude of other benefits too, such as allowing researchers to schedule the peer review process to overcome any time constraints with Stage 1 acceptance (which is sometimes noted as a barrier to their implementation). See, you're gaining information hot off the press!

But can Registered Reports combat the replication crisis? First, let's turn to their proposed benefits. The bar for acceptance of Registered Reports is arguably higher than for many standard journals, with researchers specifying high-powered research designs and appropriate statistical analyses. This overcomes issues of *underpowered research* and reduces the chance of both Type I (false positive) and Type II (false negative) errors. Similarly, Registered Reports take the focus away from *p-values* because researchers are now rewarded for robust methodology rather than their results, and are asked to implement some additional tests to assess the level of support for their hypotheses (e.g. Bayesian analyses or equivalence tests; see Lakens et al. 2018b, 2020). Furthermore, Registered Reports are proposed to increase replicability and reproducibility because the vetted protocols contain sufficient detail and, by detaching authors from their results, this should mitigate *QRPs*. Because reviewers actually evaluate the preregistration in the form of a Stage 1 proposal and then evaluate the final Stage 2 manuscript, they can spot any deviations or errors before they appear in the published literature, which can make science more *self-correcting* (Hardwicke and Ioannidis 2018). They also help to mitigate *publication bias* and the *file drawer problem* because positive, null and even inconclusive results are published. And finally, they *incentivize replication*, with a special category known as '***Registered Replication Reports***' (Nosek and Lakens 2014; Simons et al. 2014), which combine the results of numerous replications across independent labs. Woah, they seem to do it all!

How are Registered Reports faring? Do they work? Well, it's early days yet, but empirical evidence suggests that they do. Scheel et al. (2021) found that while 95 per cent of the standard (non-preregistered) literature found support for a primary hypothesis, this decreased to 44 per cent in Registered Reports. Similar findings have been found for Registered Reports across different research disciplines (Allen and Mehler 2019). At first glance, it might therefore seem that Registered Reports can combat QRPs and publication bias, but we also need to remain mindful of an alternative explanation: researchers may use this format to test riskier hypotheses (Chambers and Tzavella 2021).

Given the incentive structures that still govern academia, however, some authors worry that Registered Reports may be less often cited and that the research in them might be judged as less important and creative. Both of these worries appear to be unsupported. One preliminary analysis of 70 Registered Reports found that they are cited at either the same or a slightly higher rate than traditional articles (Hummer et al. 2017) and another suggests that when Registered Reports are concealed and compared to standard articles, peer reviewers judge them as being higher in rigour, quality and detail, as well as comparable in creativity and importance (Soderberg et al. 2021). Research also suggests that Registered Reports are more reproducible than standard articles: Obels et al. (2020) found that, out of 62 Registered Reports published between 2014 and 2018, they were able to computationally reproduce the results of 58 per cent. This is considerably higher than for journals that mandate an open data sharing policy (Hardwicke et al. 2018), but it is clearly not perfect. Initiatives are therefore under way to improve this further (Chambers and Tzavella 2021), with many journals signing up to the *Transparency and Openness Promotion* (TOP) guidelines, which are a set of standards to aid the transparency and reproducibility of published research (Nosek et al. 2015). This includes ensuring the implementation of another open science practice ...

Open materials, code and data

It's as simple as it sounds: if researchers made their research materials, analytic code and (anonymized) data available, then this would greatly aid reproducibility and replication. The term *open materials* is defined as the public sharing of inputs to a research study, such as questionnaire items, stimulus materials or experiment scripts (Kidwell et al. 2016; Parsons et al. 2022). *Open code* refers to making the computer code, such as that used in experimental programming and/or data analysis, freely and publicly available (Easterbrook 2014; Parsons et al. 2022). Finally, *open data* refers to making anonymized research data – the output – freely and publicly accessible for use by others without restrictions (Parsons et al. 2022). Together, open materials, code and data, along with best practices for their implementation, can help to make research 'FAIR' – Findable, Accessible, Interoperable and Reusable (Wilkinson et al. 2016). Of course, in sharing such information it is paramount for researchers to follow ethical guidelines, data protection laws and copyright licensing (see Chapter 5), and I aspire to the excellent saying 'as open as possible, as closed as necessary' (European Commission 2016). Nevertheless, when these practices are implemented appropriately, their positive impact on science is undeniable.

Open materials, code and data allow other researchers to 'look under the hood' of a research study, and can deter some *QRPs* and *fraud*, or make both more detectable (Rouder 2016; Vazire 2019). They also eliminate *closed science* to foster comprehensive reporting of methodology and analyses (Nosek et al. 2021), and can allow errors to be identified to make science *self-correcting*. Moreover, they can future-proof research, with detailed documentation aiding *reproducibility* and *replication* for years to come (Kathawalla et al. 2021). As well as improving science, sharing materials, code and data also offers additional benefits to researchers themselves. For example, open data is associated with more citations (Colavizza et al. 2020; McKiernan et al. 2016; Piwowar and Vision 2013), and through data reuse, it can lead to collaboration and public impact (Colavizza et al. 2020; Levenstein and Lyle 2018). Nevertheless, some researchers perceive time as the biggest barrier to implementing such best practices (Zečević et al. 2021), and my reply here would mirror that of Frith (2020) – we need to adopt *slow science* to ensure the replicability, reproducibility and credibility of our discipline.

Meta-research

We would not have been able to get to where we are now, in a period of deep reflection and scientific reform, without the discipline of meta-research. Meta-research is defined as the study of research itself, including its methods, reporting, reproducibility, evaluation and incentives (Ioannidis 2018). It has roots at the very beginning of the scientific method, with philosophers such as Francis Bacon arguing for more openness and collaboration. However, such arguments were not underpinned by systematic empirical research until recently, when the replication crisis gave rise to the meta-research discipline (Hardwicke et al. 2020). This section is deliberately short because meta-research has been interwoven throughout these pages, for example informing us of how researchers have engaged in QRPs driven by incentive structures to provide one explanation for the replication crisis (John et al. 2012), and evaluating the effectiveness of open science initiatives such as preregistration (e.g. TARG Meta-Research Group and Collaborators 2022) and Registered Reports (e.g. Scheel et al. 2021). But it rightly deserves this section of its own. This is because meta-research can help calibrate the research ecosystem towards higher standards by developing and providing empirical evidence for the many proposed reform initiatives (Hardwicke et al. 2020). By understanding the replication crisis and open science reform, perhaps you could conduct meta-research and improve the research landscape!

Big team science

Now we have discussed open science practices, I want to turn to other ways of working that can further improve reproducibility and replication. What if I told you that one solution to the problems we are seeing is simply to work together? How wonderful and simple would that be? Well, it's true! ***Big team science*** involves open, large-scale collaboration between researchers, who work together to solve fundamental research questions and pool resources across different labs, institutions, disciplines, cultures and continents (Forscher et al. 2022; Lieck 2022). This way of working has a long history in other scientific disciplines, such as physics, where huge teams work together to replicate and reproduce findings before a study is approved for publication (Junk and Lyons 2020). However, in psychological science this has been extremely rare, leading many psychologists (including myself) to argue that we need to adopt the workings of the natural sciences (Chartier et al. 2018; Forscher et al. 2022; Pennington et al. 2022).

As we saw in Chapter 2, one recent example of big team science is that of *Many Labs*, led by the Open Science Collaboration (e.g. Ebersole et al. 2016a; Klein et al. 2014). Demonstrating the scale of these efforts, Klein and 50 other authors (2014) tested the replicability of 13 psychological effects across 36 independent samples and 6344 participants. Just take a moment to soak up those numbers. Soon after came the *Reproducibility Project: Psychology*, which brought together 270 authors (Open Science Collaboration 2015). Enthused by these efforts, many other large-scale collaborations have evolved in developmental (*ManyBabies*; Frank et al. 2020) and educational psychology (*ManyClasses*; Fyfe et al. 2021), animal ecology (*ManyPrimates*; Altschul et al. 2019) and neuroscience (*#EEGManyLabs*; Pavlov et al. 2021; for an excellent overview see Lieck and Lakens 2022).

A second initiative is that of the *Psychological Science Accelerator* (PSA; Moshontz et al. 2018), which was created to facilitate generalizable and reproducible research to bridge the gap between the truth about human behaviour and our current understanding. Currently, the PSA includes a team of over 1400 researchers from 300 laboratories and 82 countries. In their recent work, the PSA has investigated the effectiveness of emotion regulation, a cognitive reappraisal strategy, in reducing negative emotions associated with the COVID-19 pandemic in over 20,000 participants across 87 countries (Wang et al. 2021), as well as examining the cultural generalizability of face perception theories in over 10,000 participants across 41 countries and 11 world regions (B.C. Jones et al. 2021). What do you notice about these initiatives? Such large-scale, transformative research cannot be achieved by a single researcher or a small team. To truly answer questions about human behaviour, we need to be able to collect large, reliable samples and ensure that both researchers and participants reflect the beautiful diversity of the human race.

But there is still a paradox when it comes to teaching and research training, with the current system of research supervision focusing on novelty and independent contribution. This means that students typically undertake individual research projects without research funding and under very strict time constraints. Given these limited resources, student projects are often small and suffer from many of the problems we see in the broader scientific literature, such as low statistical power to detect genuine effects and the increased likelihood of finding false effects (Button et al. 2016, 2020). One solution then is to adopt a big team science approach to research training and education. One student-centred initiative that embeds teaching on open and reproducible science is the *Collaborative Replications and Education Project* (CREP; Wagge et al. 2019a). Within CREP, undergraduate students are taught the best scientific practices to help them conduct high-quality direct replications of psychological research. Not only is this transformative to the students' learning process, but their involvement leads to academic publications which can greatly enhance their career and educational pathways (e.g. Ghelfi et al. 2020; Wagge et al. 2019b). Similarly, Dr Gilad Feldman, an academic at Hong Kong University, leads the Mass Replications and Extensions project, having completed over 100 replication projects with undergraduate and postgraduate students. Again, through compiled expertise and by capitalizing on diverse skill sets, this initiative produces high-quality research outputs that are published in leading academic journals (e.g. Ziano et al. 2021).

A similar approach is for supervisors to adopt, and for students to get involved in, group-based consortium projects for empirical dissertations (see Button et al. 2020; Pennington et al. 2022). This is something I am involved in, working alongside supervisors from the UK universities of Bath, Cardiff, Liverpool and Bristol. Together the supervisory team comes up with a scientifically valid research question with plausible hypotheses, and an initial outline of a robust methodology and appropriate analyses. We then advertise this project to dissertation students and work alongside each other to iteratively improve the research protocol and allow them to contribute their own research questions. The process can be seen in Figure 4.3, and throughout we embed steps to ensure that this meets degree accreditation standards (e.g. British Psychological Society 2019). Once we have developed the idea, we then train our students in reproducible big team science: together we initiate a preregistration plan with all contributors included as co-authors, and upload study materials through the centralized Open Science Framework (OSF; www.osf.io). During this stage, students also undertake various tasks, such as developing their ethics application, creating study materials and piloting experimental tasks. Importantly, they each contribute to data collection efforts, with each given a target sample size, and the samples are then pooled to ensure high-powered designs that can sufficiently answer the research questions. At the end of the project, the students write up their dissertations independently and the lead supervisor prepares the manuscript for publication (e.g. Adams et al. 2021; Tzavella et al. 2021).

Big team science boasts numerous pedagogical and scientific benefits. First, pooling available resources, which can vary from diverse expertise to funding to time, allows researchers to undertake more rigorous and reliable larger-scale studies than is normally achievable (Forscher et al. 2022; Pennington et al. 2022). This can help overcome issues of *low statistical power* to detect more reliable effects and reduce research waste. Second, big team science can reduce *QRPs* because it typically embeds open science practices from the get-go, such as preregistration and/or Registered Reports to improve transparency. They can also aid *replication* and *reproducibility* both through the standardization

Figure 4.3 A consortium approach to student research projects. Degree-accredited standards underpin each step, allowing autonomy and individual contributions while strengthening scientific rigour

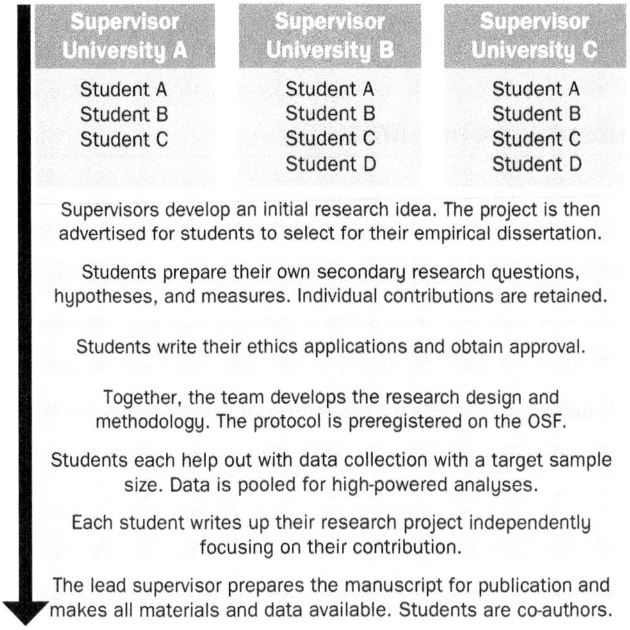

Supervisor University A	Supervisor University B	Supervisor University C
Student A	Student A	Student A
Student B	Student B	Student B
Student C	Student C	Student C
	Student D	Student D

Supervisors develop an initial research idea. The project is then advertised for students to select for their empirical dissertation.

Students prepare their own secondary research questions, hypotheses, and measures. Individual contributions are retained.

Students write their ethics applications and obtain approval.

Together, the team develops the research design and methodology. The protocol is preregistered on the OSF.

Students each help out with data collection with a target sample size. Data is pooled for high-powered analyses.

Each student writes up their research project independently focusing on their contribution.

The lead supervisor prepares the manuscript for publication and makes all materials and data available. Students are co-authors.

of methods and the need for clear communication of research procedures across labs, but also through *incentivizing replication* (e.g. CREP; Wagge et al. 2019a). Moreover, adopting open materials, code and data enables science to be *self-correcting* and future-proof.

But perhaps the most powerful benefit, which no other open science practice can foster in of itself, is the ability of big team science to increase the diversity and representation of participants and researchers. At the start of this chapter, I explained that an expanded definition of open science includes increasing its *diversity, representation* and *equality* (e.g. Ledgerwood et al. 2022). For example, in our consortium approach to the undergraduate dissertation, students with a range of diverse skill sets are welcomed onto the project and we work together on research that is of a publishable standard. In addition to providing excellent research training, this increases the variety of expertise, voices and ideas in science, helps to unearth the 'hidden curriculum' around research (e.g. learning about the publication process) and enables more students to try out a research career (Pennington et al. 2022; Strand and Brown 2019). Furthermore, by working across different labs and teams, science can become more equitable because resources can simply be shared. This model can be transformative for students who wish to pursue a career in research, but also holds benefits for those who do not. 'Open scholarship' of this kind helps students to become consumers of research who can evaluate sources critically and understand the importance of transparency (see Azevedo et al. 2022; Chopik et al. 2018). In this way, the integration of teaching with open and reproducible scholarship provides students with the necessary tools to promote long-lasting engagement with science (and I hope that this book achieves that, too!)

Open science communities

An offshoot of big team science is open science communities. These are usually bottom-up, grassroots learning groups that discuss open science in an accessible and constructive manner (Armeni et al. 2021). One example is the *ReproducibiliTEA journal clubs*, which were initiated at the University of Oxford in 2018 and have since grown across 140 institutions in 26 countries. This journal club initiative is volunteer-led and has the goal of creating a supportive and constructive community for researchers and students to keep up to date with research around reproducibility, research practice, social justice and inclusion, as well as ideas for further improving science.

Another example is the *Society for the Improvement of Psychological Science (SIPS)*, which was founded to create a community for those wanting to improve methods and practices in psychology and beyond (Steltenpohl et al. 2021). To change the traditional incentive structures of academia, SIPS awards prizes to projects that improve research training and practices, and they also develop and evaluate policies that aim to change research norms. Yet another fantastic community-driven organization is the *Framework for Open and Reproducible Research Training* (FORRT; Azevedo et al. 2019). FORRT was established in 2018 and is underpinned by the goal to embed the teaching of open and reproducible practices into higher education. Using the big team science approach in teaching, FORRT develops *open educational resources* (OERs) to reduce the labour associated with developing and implementing open scholarship content. FORRT has, for example, developed a helpful glossary of open scholarship terms (Parsons et al. 2022), a bank of lesson plans (Pownall et al. 2021) and a curated list of replications (see Azevedo et al. 2019).

Bottom-up communities have also joined hands with top-down organizations and stakeholders, such as university management, journals, funders, charities, research councils and professional bodies. For example, the *UK Reproducibility Network* (UKRN; https://www.ukrn.org/) aims to lead coordinated efforts to improve reproducibility and research integrity. The UKRN is led by a steering group of researchers from the universities of Bristol, Cardiff, Oxford and Edinburgh, who report to three other groups: Local Network Leads, Institutional Leads and a Stakeholders Engagement Group. Local Network Leads are grassroots volunteers who represent the UKRN for their university or research institute, and provide support and training to other researchers. Many universities also have Institutional Leads who have a formal role within senior management. Lastly, stakeholders engage with the UKRN to support their initiatives and assess ways to improve research culture. The UKRN was established in 2019 and has since grown globally, with additional Reproducibility

Networks forming in Australia, Germany, Switzerland and Finland, to name just a few (UKRN Steering Committee 2021).

Challenges to open science

Although open science brings with it many advantages, it also has its own challenges. Here I discuss two of these that need to be continually monitored for open science to achieve its potential of research reform.

The first challenge is to overturn deep-rooted incentive structures in academic culture. We have seen numerous examples of open science initiatives that have been developed by researchers, highlighting that many want to see positive change. But to fully succeed, researchers need to be supported by their institutions, funders, publishers and the government. If science does not change so that what is good for the scientist is also good for science, then these problems will live on. Thankfully, it seems that sustained change is indeed taking effect. For example, some journals have implemented a 'badge' system, which is a strategy developed by the Center for Open Science that attaches a visual icon to research articles to certify that a study has been preregistered or shares its materials and/or data (Kidwell et al. 2016). Some funders have also mandated open access publications and recognize the benefits of preprints (Armeni et al. 2021), and others have partnered with journals to offer funding for Registered Reports (UKRN Steering Committee 2021). Excitingly, in 2021, the UK House of Commons launched a parliamentary inquiry into reproducibility and research integrity. Responses included voices from the UKRN, who argued that institutions must realign hiring and progression policies to acknowledge open, transparent and slow science (Stewart et al. 2022), and from FORRT, who proposed that the government should support open science communities to improve research training and education (Azevedo et al. 2022). The European Commission has also developed the *Open Science Agenda* for 2025, which focuses on open access scholarly outputs, FAIR research data and changing institutional research assessments (European University Association 2022).

Perhaps the biggest challenge facing open science, however, is ensuring equality, diversity and representation (Murphy et al. 2020; Pownall et al. 2021; Whitaker and Guest 2020). Open science needs to be more than practices, but also about who is sitting around, and welcomed, to the table (Ledgerwood et al. 2022). In these moments of change, we need to address a historic lack of diversity and non-inclusive culture in research. As practised in Western culture, psychological science was created for and drew on the experiences of White, affluent males (Ledgerwood et al. 2022) and, if like its history, open science reform also prioritizes such views then it risks excluding many talented individuals who may feel overwhelmed, unwelcome or excluded (Murphy et al. 2020; Whitaker and Guest 2020). To overcome this challenge, we need an expansive vision for open science which includes diversifying who defines it and reorders traditional power dynamics. What would this look like? Well, an inclusive open science would champion all voices equitably, consider the systemic marginalization that some individuals face, and work to dismantle pervasive hierarchies in academia (Pownall et al. 2021).

So now, at the end of this chapter, let's regroup to assess where open science is at. Open science incorporates many new and exciting practices to reform psychological science, and with it, we are seeing clear improvements in transparency, rigour and reproducibility. No one open science practice is a panacea, however, and not all practices will work for every research project. I share the view of others in suggesting that there is no perfect way to do open science, and engaging in at least one practice makes you an open scientist (Bergmann 2018; Crüwell et al. 2019; Kathawalla et al. 2021). You may be thinking that there is so much to learn, and this can feel overwhelming. Don't worry, I am not going to leave you here! In Chapter 5, I will provide you with a beginner's guide to implementing open science practices – whether you are a student wanting to embed them in your own research or a teacher wanting to impart such knowledge to the next generation of researchers. But before we jump in, I want to leave you with this: recent research has shown that when open science *is* practiced, we can overcome replication concerns (Protzko et al. 2020), and, in the case of the COVID-19 pandemic, open science may even save lives (Besançon et al. 2021). I hope you share my excitement about the good that open science can bring to our discipline (and beyond). Buckle up as I now show you how to implement this for yourself!

Activity: Answer the questions to complete the crossword and test your knowledge of open science!

Down

1 What is the 'gold-standard' practice of preregistration?
2 What is the practice that allows other researchers to verify the findings of research?
3 Large-scale collaboration between labs, institutions, disciplines, cultures and continents is known as _____?
4 Which UK open science community brings together Local Network Leads, Institutional Leads and stakeholders to promote reproducible and transparent research practices?

Across

5 The expanded definition of open science includes increasing diversity, representation and _____.
6 What practice involves a researcher uploading their experimental programming script to a public repository?
7 Open science practices can aid replication and _____.
8 What open science practice requires researchers to initiate a time-stamped, read-only document of their research plans?
9 What is the name of a scientific document posted before peer review on a trusted internet repository?

5 | A student's guide to open science

> The first principle is that you must not fool yourself – and you are the easiest person to fool.
>
> (Feynman 1974)

This chapter provides a beginner's guide to implementing open science practices in your research workflow. Echoing Bergmann (2018), it's helpful to see open science as a buffet: you don't need to learn all of these practices overnight, but rather you can pick and choose as and when you need them. As time goes on, and you feel comfortable with each practice, you can then build on your expertise and use your open science toolkit. At this stage, it is also worth remembering that open science does not prescribe a specific set of rules, but instead should be seen as a collection of behaviours (Corker 2018; Norris and O'Connor 2019). As such, not all of these practices will always be relevant or possible for your work, and you can decide which are best for you. In the spirit of big team science, I also encourage you to talk to your supervisors, collaborators, peers, ethics board and librarians about open science practices; this way, you can check that they are appropriate for the study you are planning and feel reassured that everyone is on the same page.

At this point, I also want to (re)state that I am an experimental, quantitative psychologist, so many of the examples here are naturally based on my expertise. For this reason, I signpost you to some additional excellent guides on embedding open science in qualitative research, which include resources on preregistration (Haven and van Grootel 2019; Haven et al. 2020), open data (Branney et al. 2019; Karhulahti 2022) and big team science (Richards and Hemphill 2017). I also recommend many accessible general guides to open science in Table 5.1. Last but certainly not least, the FORRT team have developed the most helpful community-sourced glossary of over 100 open scholarship terms (Parsons et al. 2022), which is continuously being updated.

You may be feeling overwhelmed by the many new practices proposed in Chapter 4 and may be worried about the time and effort required to learn them (I felt the same when embarking on my open science journey). I want you to take a moment to reflect on why it's important to embed open science in research. By now I hope I have convinced you about the need for improved transparency, replicability and reproducibility in psychological science and beyond. Open science is therefore good for science and there are numerous unselfish reasons to adopt these practices, such as disseminating reliable and

Table 5.1 A recap of open science practices, along with helpful resources

Practice	Definition	Resources
Open science	An umbrella term reflecting the idea that knowledge should be openly accessible, transparent, rigorous, reproducible and replicable. It encapsulates the practices of open access and preprints, study preregistration, Registered Reports, and open materials, code and data. Open science also includes confronting all biases with consideration of diversity, equality and representation in science.	Allen and Mehler (2019); Bartlett and Eaves (2019); Kathawalla et al. (2021); Klein et al. (2018a); Ledgerwood et al. (2022); Murphy et al. (2020); Robson et al. (2021)
Preprint	A scientific document made available legally outside of a traditional publisher by posting it online in a trusted internet repository (e.g. PsyArXiv).	Moshontz et al. (2021); Spitschan et al. (2020)
Preregistration	Registering a study protocol, including the research questions, hypotheses, design, variables and data analysis plan, before data collection and/or analysis. It should be uploaded to a verified repository (e.g. https://osf.io/prereg/), ensuring that it is date/time-stamped, permanent and publicly available.	Haven and van Grootel (2019); Haven et al. (2020); Merten and Krypotos (2019); van den Akker et al. (2021a)
Registered Report	A publishing format where initial peer review is performed on a study protocol before data collection and/or analyses are conducted. Peer review is split into two stages: pre-study (Stage 1) and post-study (Stage 2). Accepted Stage 1 manuscripts are given 'in principle acceptance' (IPA), moving the focus to the process of research and away from the results.	Chambers and Tzavella, (2021); Field (2020); Kiyonaga and Scimeca (2019); Stewart et al. (2020); https://www.cos.io/rr
Open materials	Making study materials (e.g. questionnaires, experimental tasks, interviews) publicly available to facilitate reproducibility and reuse.	Gilmore et al. (2018)
Open code	Making computer code (e.g. programming, analysis code) publicly available to make research methodology and analysis transparent and facilitate reproducibility.	Soderberg (2018)
Open data	Making data publicly available for viewing, reproduction and reuse. Open data must uphold ethical considerations (e.g. participant anonymity). Also known as data sharing.	Meyer (2018); Turner et al. (2020); Ross et al. (2018); Rouder (2016); Walsh et al. (2018)

robust information, increasing trust in research, not being gatekeepers of knowledge, helping other people to use and build on research products, ensuring that mistakes can be identified and allowing readers to properly evaluate research and reflect on its limitations (Kathawalla et al. 2021). But there are also many selfish reasons, with practices such as preprints allowing you to disseminate your work earlier to gain feedback, preregistration encouraging you to better plan out your research, and sharing materials, code and data that can future-proof your work. Furthermore, it's important to learn about these practices because they are increasingly being discussed and adopted. For example, study preregistration is now a prerequisite in the undergraduate dissertation stage of some UK psychology degrees, with others even trying their hands at Registered Reports (Button et al. 2016, 2020; Blincoe and Buchert 2020; Pownall 2020). Many PhD and postdoctoral students are also paving the way with the implementation of open science practices in their research degrees (e.g. Henderson et al. 2021; Leganes-Fonteneau et al. 2021; Mol et al. 2022). Figure 5.1 outlines where in the research process you might embed these different practices.

Figure 5.1 Embedding open science in your research workflow

Platforms to facilitate open science: using the OSF

Before I outline specific open science practices, it's good to think more generally about the platforms and resources that can help you on your way. There are many avenues to share aspects of your research workflow, such as via personal, laboratory and project-specific websites, institutional repositories, data repositories (e.g. UK Data Service) and supplementary materials attached to published articles and/or assessments. However, these different platforms might only allow you to share specific things (e.g. data) and some may not be seen as verified platforms for certain practices (e.g. preregistration). One platform that solves this problem, allowing you to store all aspects of your research in one place, is the *Open Science Framework* (OSF). The OSF was developed by the not-for-profit *Center for Open Science*, whose mission is to increase openness, integrity and reproducibility in scholarly research. Through easy-to-navigate project folders, users can upload preprints, initiate study preregistration and Registered Reports, and share their materials, code and data. There are many great things about the OSF, but perhaps the most useful are that it provides version control and transparently documents project updates, stores data under local legislation (e.g. the General Data Protection Regulation for the EU; see Klein et al. 2018a), and uses persistent and unique identifiers (e.g. DOIs) to allow for discoverability and citation.

Signing up and using the OSF is simple. You just need to visit https://osf.io and click on the green 'Sign up' button. Once you have an account, you will then be directed to a home page where you can search the entire OSF database for other research projects or navigate to the tab titled 'My projects' to start adding your own. To practise, you could create a private, mock project by clicking 'Create project', filling in the necessary boxes and adding different folders. For example, you may want folders for your research materials, data or code. Before you share, if the research is not your own (e.g. you wish to share research materials originally used by another researcher), be sure to check the licensing and copyright, which I will return to later in the section on 'open materials, code and data'. Having created your mock project, you can then tinker around with the OSF without being worried about making mistakes. Once you feel confident, you can create real folders and toggle between the private (when you are not yet ready to release your project to other users) and public settings (when you are). When creating such projects for real, you should ensure that your folder names and the files within them are understandable and clear (it's not just you who might look at them). And when you come to write up your research project for an assessment or even publication, you can include a direct link to your OSF project page.

Sharing your research workflow on the OSF increases the likelihood that your work can easily be found and reused by others, and helps to preserve it in the long term (no 'the dog ate my dissertation' excuses!). Furthermore, sharing so much information about your project relieves the stresses of answering individual requests, sifting through multiple computer folders or misplacing something entirely (Gilmore et al. 2018). The OSF can protect past you from future you! But remember, you are in control of what you wish to share and when it is best to do so, and so a useful phrase to always keep in mind is 'as open as possible, as closed as necessary' (European Commission 2016). My first recommendation for implementing open science practices into your workflow is to simply sign up and learn to use the OSF.

Preprints

One way to facilitate the discoverability of your research is to make it open access. There are two main routes: the gold route refers to open access via a publisher, with most still charging an Article Processing Charge (APC), while the green route refers to authors self-archiving their work (Bourne et al. 2017; Crüwell et al. 2019). With regard to green open access, *preprint servers* allow researchers to upload, describe and disseminate their work, legally, for free (see Moshontz et al. 2021; Spitschan et al. 2020). This can include research manuscripts that have not yet been submitted for peer review, those under review at a journal, or even author-formatted versions of accepted articles before publication. Kathawalla et al. (2021) rate article preprints as perhaps the lowest effort open science practice that you can implement.

Before uploading your work to a preprint server there are some important decisions that you need to make. First, you will want to choose a licence for your work so that others know how they should use it. Let's take the preprint server *PsyArXiv*, for example. This server supports the 'CC0 1.0 Universal' licence, which places work in the public domain, and the 'CC-BY' licence, which allows others to reuse and build on your work under the agreement that they give you (the original author) credit (they cite your work). The Creative Commons website (https://creativecommons.org) helps you to decide which is the best licence for your work, with many authors selecting the CC-BY licence to retain the copyright of their work while allowing other people to use it freely (Bourne et al. 2017; Kathawalla et al. 2021).

Second, if your end goal is to submit your work to a journal, you will need to check their rules for 'internet posting'; most journals allow for the posting of preprints before submission, as well as the author's final version of the accepted article (before it goes through their proofing and editing stages, which costs them money!). Most journals, however, do not let you upload the publisher-formatted version unless you've paid the 'APC' to retain copyright (Moshontz et al. 2021). You can easily find this information by either reading through your chosen journal's guidelines, or checking on the wonderful Sherpa Romeo website (https://v2.sherpa.ac.uk/romeo/), which tracks the preprint policies of publishers. Once you have done this, be sure to include some information about the status of the preprint on the title page (e.g. 'Not yet submitted for publication', 'Submitted for publication', 'Resubmitted for publication' or 'Published'), along with the version number and date (Moshontz et al. 2021). This allows readers to understand the stage of the research and, perhaps more importantly, other people who discover your work to report on it appropriately (e.g. by warning readers to exercise caution in the case of non-peer-reviewed preprints). In addition, be sure to include any information that the specific journal may require. Finally, before posting, check that your co-authors or supervisory team approve of the preprint being submitted.

After following these steps, you should next choose a preprint server that's hosted in a stable and public location, such as an institutional or scholarly repository that is designed to host preprints (Moshontz et al. 2021). Table 5.2 provides some examples. All preprint servers only accept submissions from registered authors, so you first need to sign up and follow their instructions to post your preprint. The majority of these servers allow you to directly upload a Word document, which is then converted to a PDF. When you upload your preprint, the server will take you through step-by-step instructions to provide some meta-data (e.g. Title, Abstract), which will make your work discoverable. Voila! After following these steps and the top tips (see the top tips box), you will have your very first preprint!

Study preregistration

Throughout a typical research study, researchers have to make lots of different decisions – how many participants should be collected? What inclusion or exclusion criteria are needed? What dependent variables should be used? What analyses are most appropriate? As I discussed in Chapter 4, this leaves a lot of room for 'researcher degrees of freedom' – self-serving biases that affect our decisions. If these decisions are made *after* collecting or analysing the data, then we submerge ourselves in hot water: these decisions can begin to influence the findings, rather than the data itself!

Table 5.2   Example preprint servers across different research disciplines

Preprint server	Discipline	Link
PsyArXiv	Psychology	https://psyarxiv.com/
arXiv	Natural sciences, engineering, economics, computing	https://arxiv.org/
bioRxiv	Biology	https://www.biorxiv.org/
SocArXiv	Social sciences	https://osf.io/preprints/socarxiv/
SSRN	Social sciences	https://ssrn.com/en
MetaArXiv	Meta-research, transparency and reproducibility	https://osf.io/preprints/metaarxiv/
EdArXiv	Education research	https://edarxiv.org/
AfricArXiv	African research	https://info.africarxiv.org/
AgrRxiv	Agriculture and allied sciences	https://agrirxiv.org/
F1000 Research	Life sciences	https://f1000research.com/
Thesis Commons	Dissertations/theses	https://thesiscommons.org/
OSF Preprints	Collates preprints across disciplines	https://osf.io/preprints/

Top tips for preprints

1 Be sure you're ready for other people to read your manuscript: give the final version a thorough proofread and make sure it's formatted well.

2 Make sure your research team is aware and approves of posting the preprint.

3 Do not upload confidential or participant-identifying information to preprint servers: follow ethical guidelines for all open science practices.

4 Think about the licensing you want to use: Creative Commons provides a great guide (https://creativecommons.org/).

5 If you plan to submit to a journal, check their guidelines or use the helpful Sherpa Romeo guide (https://v2.sherpa.ac.uk/romeo/). In your cover letter to the journal, state that you have uploaded the article as a preprint.

6 Include the date of the preprint version on the title page, along with its status (i.e. 'Not submitted for publication', 'Submitted for publication', 'Under review', etc.).

7 Update your preprint after revising it (making sure to change its version number and status too). If published, replace with the author accepted version (but recap points 4 and 5 above).

8 If an article is corrected or even retracted, this should be reflected in the preprint too.

Recall that preregistration is the act of registering a study protocol – the research questions, hypotheses, design, variables and data analysis plan – before data collection and/or analysis. At this point, you may be thinking: 'But hold on a minute, I typically do this when I submit my study to an ethical review board?' You're partly right, but the key difference is that a preregistration is uploaded to a verified repository, which ensures that it is date/time-stamped, permanent and publicly accessible. You can preregister your study on many different platforms, such as the OSF (www.osf.io), AsPredicted (https://aspredicted.org/) or, if it's a clinical study, ClinicalTrials.Gov. The first step, then, is to decide what type of study you are conducting, and where's the best place to preregister. Table 5.3 provides a summary of preregistration templates for you to explore, and a recent paper by Haroz (2022) compares and contrasts different repositories.

Once you have chosen your template, you can then start working through it. Let's take the example of preregistering an experimental, quantitative study. Many templates will ask you to provide your hypotheses, as well as detailed information about the planned sample size and rules for stopping data collection, the research materials (e.g. experimental measures, questionnaires), participant inclusion and exclusion criteria, how your dependent variables are computed and the data analysis strategy. With regard to your hypotheses, it is best to number them and separate each one to make sure they are not ambiguous. Furthermore, it is important to check that your analysis plan allows you to appropriately test these hypotheses (ensuring synergy between the different components of your preregistration). One of the most important things is to be specific.

To make preregistration more concrete, let's take a look at the AsPredicted. org template. I started with this myself to build my confidence, and then progressed up to the OSF standard preregistration template, which is more detailed and comprehensive (which is what you want from a preregistration!). The AsPredicted template asks the following eight questions:

Template from AsPredicted (https://aspredicted.org/)

1 Have any data been collected for this study already?
2 What's the main question being asked or hypothesis being tested in this study?
3 Describe the key dependent variable(s) specifying how they will be measured.
4 How many and which conditions will participants be assigned to?
5 Specify exactly which analyses you will conduct to examine the main question/hypothesis.
6 Describe exactly how outliers will be defined and handled, and your precise rule(s) for excluding observations.
7 How many observations will be collected or what will determine sample size? No need to justify decision, but be precise about exactly how the number will be determined.
8 Anything else you would like to pre-register? (e.g. secondary analyses, variables collected for exploratory purposes, unusual analyses planned?).

Table 5.3 Example preregistration templates

Template	Intended use	Link	Resources
AsPredicted.org	Quantitative/experimental studies	https://aspredicted.org	Simmons et al. (2018, 2020a)
OSF Prereg*	Quantitative/experimental studies	https://osf.io/zab38/wiki/home/	Bowman et al. (2020)
PRP-Quant	Quantitative/experimental studies	https://www.psycharchives.org/en/item/088c79cb-237c-4545-a9e2-3616d6cc8453	Bosnjak et al. (2022)
Secondary data preregistration	Existing data/quantitative	https://osf.io/jqxfz/	van den Akker et al. (2021a)
fMRI preregistration	fMRI data design	https://osf.io/dvb2e/	Beyer et al. (2021)
Replication Recipe	Replication studies	https://osf.io/zab38/wiki/home/	Brandt et al. (2014)
Preregistration in social psychology	Quantitative/experimental social psychology	https://osf.io/k5wns/	van 't Veer and Giner-Sorolla (2016)
Cognitive modelling	Quantitative: cognitive models	https://doi.org/10.6084/m9.figshare.16665981.v1	Crüwell and Evans (2021)
Qualitative preregistration	Qualitative studies	https://osf.io/zab38/wiki/home/	Haven and van Grootel (2019); Haven et al. (2020)
Systematic reviews	Systematic literature reviews of human and animal studies	https://www.crd.york.ac.uk/prospero/	Page et al. (2018); Stewart et al. (2012)

*This is the OSF's standard preregistration template, but they offer many alternatives.

The best way of writing a high-quality preregistration is to liken it to a cake recipe: if one step is missing and a person tries to follow it, then they will end up with a drastically different cake (including the shape, size and taste!). Just like writing a step-by-step recipe, you need to include detail in your preregistration, justifying the decisions you have made. Using the AsPredicted template above, you would want to ensure that you have explained the following: What is the background that underpins your research questions? What is your specific dependent variable, what is it made up of, and how is it computed? What is your rationale for your sample size? (See Lakens 2022 for an excellent guide.) Now before you finalize it, think: if you gave this to someone else, would they be able to follow it from start to finish? Preregistration should take time and care; it's not a tick-box exercise, and if you treat it as such, you'll only be annoyed at yourself later down the line!

As you develop your open science skills, you might look back at an older preregistration and think 'Oops! That doesn't sound great, it could have been so much better!' This is the natural process of learning – I look back at my first preregistration and realize that it was underspecified in some areas and not as detailed as it could have been. The key thing is to learn from these oversights and implement future improvements. Remember as well that preregistration is a plan and not a prison (DeHaven 2017); as you progress with your study, you may realize that you missed something out, or that something isn't working as planned and requires a tweak. If this happens, you can simply report this transparently in your final manuscript (e.g. including a 'deviations from preregistration' table or description), and if you initiated your preregistration via the OSF, you can now update this as you go! The key is always *transparency*. So, what are you waiting for? Have a look at my top tips and start to preregister your studies.

Top tips for study preregistration

- Assume no prior knowledge of the reader – explain variable names and how dependent variables will be calculated. Make sure descriptions are clear.
- Make sure you are specific – remember that a lot of preregistrations are underspecified; don't be one of those people! For this reason, it is best to use templates that don't have word count limitations (AsPredicted.org, for example, has limits when used via their website, but *not* when using this same template via the Open Science Framework!)

(Continued)

(Continued)
⟶

- Link any materials and/or data analysis scripts to your preregistration if you can do so.
- Work with your research team (e.g. supervisor, collaborators) to ensure you all understand the study. All collaborators should approve the preregistration submission.
- Make sure that the independent components of your preregistration are consistent – e.g. it should be clear how your analysis strategy can test the hypotheses.
- Distinguish your confirmatory (planned) and exploratory (unplanned) analyses.
- Crucially, upload your preregistration to a verified platform, ensuring that it becomes *time-stamped*, *permanent* and can be made *publicly accessible*.

In your report/article:

- Make sure you provide a link (DOI/URL) to your preregistration.
- List all of your preregistered hypotheses.
- Clearly distinguish confirmatory and exploratory hypotheses/analyses.
- Report all preregistered analyses.
- Remember that preregistration is a 'plan and not a prison'. Report deviations transparently (e.g. by reporting them in your report and/or updating your preregistration via the new 'update' feature in OSF).
- Challenge yourself to improve each preregistration as you learn.

Registered Reports

The main difference between study preregistration and Registered Reports is that the latter are submitted for peer review before data collection and/or analysis. If the proposed study receives 'in principle acceptance' (IPA), then the study is published regardless of its results, as long as the authors stick to their planned protocol and/or have ensured that any deviations were cleared by the editors. IPA gives researchers a serious advantage, because at this point a reviewer cannot point out additional 'flaws' in the study on viewing the results. While preregistration and Registered Reports encourage researchers to put in greater effort in the planning stages of research design, Registered Reports go one step further by ensuring that this protocol is checked and is iteratively improved through the peer review process.

A fantastic guide on Registered Reports is provided by Stewart et al. (2020), and the Center for Open Science keeps an updated list of journals that offer this publishing format (https://www.cos.io/initiatives/registered-reports). Many universities now teach about Registered Reports and some even use this format for assessed research projects: specifically, students design their study and submit a 'Stage 1' proposal for feedback (the Introduction and Methods), and then they collect and analyse their data before submitting their final 'Stage 2' report (the Results and Discussion).

For researchers who want to pursue this publishing format formally, the first recommendation is to think carefully about the specificity of your proposed research questions and hypotheses, and then start to build robust methods and analyses that map onto these. Second, you should think about the feasibility of your sampling plan, with consideration of any time or resource constraints. Third, you should think deeply about the validity of the proposed methods or analyses before submission, which can be guided by pilot data. To provide an example, my colleagues and I designed a Stage 1 Registered Report with three research questions and a complex analysis that we initially thought could answer these questions. However, with help from the editors and reviewers, we realized that the analysis we had chosen produced far too many comparisons. This in-depth planning stage allowed us to go back to the drawing board to think about what *exact* comparisons could stringently test our hypotheses. This shows the advantage of the peer review process, enabling you to spot and solve problems at the start rather than at the end of a study! As you work through your proposal, you should then check that there are precise links between the research questions, hypotheses, sampling and analysis plans, and outline your interpretations in the case of different outcomes. Finally, you should ensure that you have appropriate data quality checks (e.g. attention and manipulation checks; see Chambers and Tzavella 2021 for an in-depth guide).

One of the main barriers that researchers perceive around Registered Reports is time, but this can be overcome with careful planning. Arguably, Registered Reports are more time-efficient than study preregistration because in the former you have already written the Introduction and Methods and have had these approved. Also, by gaining IPA for the study before collecting your data, you prevent the need for multiple journal submissions, which are typical for traditional articles when reviewers and editors decide that they don't like the results. Remember also that the new initiative *Peer Community In Registered Reports* (https://rr.peercommunityin.org/) offers a scheduled review track, in which researchers submit a one-page 'snapshot' of their proposed research, and then request a specific time period for peer review to be conducted. Showing that time barriers can indeed be overcome, Dr Emma Henderson of Kingston University completed her entire PhD through the publication of Registered Reports!

Open materials, code and data

To aid replication (allowing other people to repeat our study) and reproducibility (allowing others to check our findings), researchers need to share materials, code and data. Without sharing materials, how do we know what question-naires, experimental measures or stimuli were used? Without sharing code, how we do know the intricate details of experimental trials, or how data was screened, cleaned and analysed? Without sharing data, how do we know how many participants were excluded before analysis or whether the reported results can be verified? Although researchers try their very best to explain these details in their research reports, there are (many) times in which they are overlooked. Why don't we just *share*?

Let's start by thinking about open materials. In some studies, the materials may comprise a list of questionnaire items or experimental scripts with code (e.g. the Stroop Task), while others may use video stimuli or even record real-world interactions (Grahe 2015; Klein et al. 2018a). Many repositories help make sharing materials easy, such as GitHub (https://github.com/), Figshare (https://figshare.com/) and the trusty OSF. If you are using materials that weren't developed by you, then it is essential that you check their copyright before sharing (remember, 'as open as possible, as closed as necessary'). For example, some materials are only available via researcher requests from the original authors and have intricate terms and conditions for reuse. If, for this valid reason, the materials cannot be shared, you can simply upload a 'README' file with an explanation along with as much information as you *can* provide (e.g. where to request access for the materials, which questionnaire items or images you used), and provide a link to this in your article. If you are creating your materials, think about the source of the software you have used and whether the end user has access: if your experimental script is programmed in open-source software (e.g. PsychoPy; Peirce et al. 2019), then anyone should be able to install this for free and view your materials. On the other hand, if it is programmed in proprietary software (e.g. Inquisit, E-prime), then others will need a paid-for licence. Even in the latter case, you can share your materials by exporting your programming code to a text file. In another scenario, suppose that you create your own experimental task or questionnaire and want to share this with others for maximum reuse; in this instance, you can release your materials under a Creative Commons licence that allows others to reuse your work while ensuring that you retain all rights as the author (Bartlett 2020; Hays et al. 2018). The OSF is great for this purpose because it allows you to link a Digital Object Identifier (DOI) to your work, select the appropriate licence, and make it public or private as appropriate. Finally, you should always adhere to ethical principles when sharing materials – if a person is identifiable in the experimental stimuli (e.g. in studies on social cognition), or in videos (e.g. observation studies), ensure that each person has consented to their image being shared and that they understand how these materials will be used. Similarly, in your ethics application, make sure you explain how you plan to share your materials and the procedures you have in place to mitigate any associated risks.

Let's now turn to open code. Perhaps confusingly, 'open code' can refer to both the code used in experimental scripts, and also the code used to screen, clean and analyse your data (*analysis scripts*). Even point-and-click analysis software, such as SPSS and JASP, is underpinned by computer code that can be shared. For example, if you are using SPSS, then you can run your analysis as usual, but before pressing the big 'OK' button to produce the results, press 'PASTE' and you will be presented with a second pop-up box that documents all of the underlying code (called *syntax*). Now you can annotate this code to make it clear to the reader which analysis did what, modify and execute this code in the future, and simply save it so that it can be shared. To help people who do not have an SPSS licence, you can also export this code to many other formats such as a Word document or text file. Similarly, analyses conducted through point-and-click options in JASP can be exported to aid reproducible analyses. It's also a good habit to get other people to check your code to identify where additional clarity could be included and to spot any errors!

Finally, you can add open data to your ever-expanding open science skills. Some of you may already have experience with data sharing or may be gearing up to implement this practice within your research workflow (e.g. in the appendices of your research reports or published works). Before setting out on your data sharing journey, however, make sure you discuss this with your supervisors and/or collaborators so that you know who will manage this activity. Furthermore, if you are in doubt about any aspect of data sharing, reach out to your ethics board and librarians, who know a lot about data management and governance. When you are ready to start sharing your data, you will need to think carefully about *ethical principles* and *data management* throughout. In your application for ethical approval, you will want to include information regarding how your data will be stored and shared, and what will happen to a participant's data should they exercise their rights to withdraw. Here you should ensure that all participant-facing ethical materials include information about open data (What is it? What does it mean?) so that participants have a clear understanding and can provide their informed consent. Below is an example of ethical materials that include open data, but you must look into the ethical guidelines of your university or research organization as these may differ considerably. You will also want to check that the place where you wish to store your data adheres to data protection laws, such as the General Data Protection Regulation for researchers in the European Union. The website www.re3data.org provides a helpful registry of research data repositories, and your supervisor, ethics board, tutors and librarians can also help you to find the one most suitable for your research.

An example of ethical materials, integrating open science practices

Participant Information Sheet

How will my data be used?
Your study data will be anonymized, and all data collected will remain confidential. This means that it will be given an identification number and we will not collect any identifying information about you.

At the end of the study your data will become 'open data'. This means that it will be stored in an online database (e.g. https://www.osf.io) so that it is

→

> publicly available. This allows other researchers to verifying the findings and/ or reuse the data.
>
> ### What is open data?
>
> Open data means that data are made available, free of charge, to anyone interested in the research, or who wishes to conduct their own analysis of the data. All data will be anonymized before it is made available, and therefore there will be no way to identify you from the research data.
>
> ### Why open data?
>
> Sharing research data and findings is considered best scientific practice and is a requirement of many funding bodies and scientific journals. As a large proportion of research is publicly funded, the outcomes of the research should be made publicly available. Sharing data helps to maximize the impact of investment through wider use and encourages new avenues of research.
>
> ### Consent Form
>
> o I have read and understood the Participant Information Sheet. **YES/NO**
>
> o I consent for my anonymized data to be made publicly available ('open data') for verification and/or reuse by other researchers. **YES/NO** ...

Next, you will want to think about *what data should be shared*. Here there is a distinction between raw data – the data as it was originally recorded (warts and all) – and processed data – the data that has been extracted and/or compiled to provide the input for your analysis. You may be thinking that you'd like to share your raw and processed data, which would be deemed best practice, but again you will need to consider research ethics and manage any associated risks (British Psychological Society 2021; Klein et al. 2018a). Specifically, it is important to ensure that participants cannot be re-identified via their shared data (Klein et al. 2018a; Ross et al. 2018), so ask yourself 'is my data anonymized to protect and preserve participants' privacy?' If the answer is 'Yes', for example you have anonymized participants with a random identifier, or if personal information was collected separately from the data you want to share, then you are likely to be able to share your raw data. If the answer is 'No', then you should take extra steps before sharing your data openly.

Even if you can't share the raw data, it is almost always possible to share anonymized data in the form that they were entered into statistical analyses (Klein et al. 2018a). For example, you could redact potentially identifying information, such as participants' demographics (see Sweeney 2000) and provide the main data that's needed to reproduce your analyses. If this is still impossible, for example your analyses are based on demographic information (e.g. age), you can also look into creating a synthetic data set that de-identifies participants while preserving the statistical properties and relationships among variables (Quintana 2020). Data sharing, as you can see, is complex and nuanced, and some data can be difficult to anonymize fully (e.g. qualitative data, neuroimaging). If, after all of these considerations, you believe that there are reasons not to share your data, then simply explain this explicitly in your research report. I want to reiterate the importance of not doing this alone: sharing data is difficult and you must seek support from your research team and tutors.

Open data also requires good data management and organization, which is a beneficial, transferable skill for any data in your life! This is important for open data because you want others to be able to understand and verify your work, as well as guaranteeing that it's future-proof. It's helpful to always have the 'FAIR' principles in mind when you decide to share your data – it should be *Findable, Accessible, Interoperable* and *Reusable* (Wilkinson et al. 2016). With regard to *Findable*, I recommend that you use a recognized data archive in your field, such as the OSF, and provide a direct link to this in your research outputs. You will then want to ensure that your data is *Accessible* – is it locked away on a private project page? Or is it locked in proprietary software where others might need a licence to access it? Make sure it is openly available by making your project page available/public and aim to convert any proprietary file types to open-source versions. Now ask yourself, is this data *Interoperable*? This means that your data (and metadata, which describes your data) should be readable by both humans and machines. In my experience, this principle is the most overlooked. Rather than dumping your data onto the OSF, check first that it's got an appropriate file name that is informative, and that the data is well structured. A great resource for file naming and data sharing is provided by Sara Bowman on the OSF (https://help.osf.io/hc/en-us/articles/360019931113-File-naming). But that's not all; next, ask yourself would a naive person be able to interpret the data in your file without you by their side explaining it? It is best practice to also upload a **data codebook** (also known as a data dictionary), which provides a list and detailed annotation of all of the variables in the data set, what they refer to and how they were compiled.

Figure 5.2 shows an example of how data can be shared using Microsoft Excel. In Panel A, you can see that the codebook explains each tab in the Excel file, and in Panel B, this same codebook then details what each variable means in the 'analysis data' tab. Again, your supervisor and/or collaborators can help you further with this because there are different conventions with data naming and sharing, which can differ between research fields and even just preference!

And finally, you need to ensure that your data meets the 'FAIR' principle of being *Reusable*. As I have discussed with open materials and code above, you should finish by attaching a licence to your data so that others know exactly how it can be reused. You are now on your way to being an open science pro!

Figure 5.2 An example data codebook

A.

	A	B
1	Tab Number	Description
2	1	Raw data: The uncleaned data downloaded from the experimental software Inquisit.
3	2	Excluded data: An overview of data exclusions with accompanying reasons for exclusion.
4	3	Analysis data: The analysed data entered into statistical software after data exclusions.

Data Codebook   1. Raw Data   2. Excluded Data   3. Analysis Data   ⊕

B.

Tab: 3. Analysis Data

Variable name	Variable description	Measurement unit	Allowed values
Participant ID	A random ID number assigned to each participant	Numeric	PP-001 to PP-019
CONDITION	Randomly assigned experimental condition, determined using a random number generator	Numeric	1 = Positive social media
SocialMedia_1	Response to question "I felt happy when reading people's Facebook statuses" (1=Strongly Disagree,	Numeric	1-7
SocialMedia_2	Response to question "I felt excited when reading people's Facebook statuses" (1=Strongly Disagree	Numeric	1-7
SocialMedia_3	Response to question "I felt sad when reading people's Facebook statuses" (1=Strongly Disagree, 7	Numeric	1-7
SocialMedia_4	Response to question "I felt nervous when reading people's Facebook statuses" (1=Strongly Disagre	Numeric	1-7
SocialMedia_5	Response to question "I felt worried when reading people's Facebook statuses" (1=Strongly Disagree	Numeric	1-7
SocialMedia_Score	Total score summed across SocialMedia_1 to SocialMedia_5	Numeric	5.35

Variable names should be identical to those in your data spreadsheet.

Define the variable with enough information for another person to understand.

Include the measurement unit (numeric, string, date...) for the variable.

Define the allowed values: the range or meaning of values accepted for the variable.

Top tips for open materials, code and data

- Communicate with your team to ensure you are all on the same page when it comes to sharing and you know when is the right time to share.
- Think carefully about ethical guidelines and data protection.
- Plan for open materials, code and data from the start of your project.
- Upload your materials, code and data to a future-proof repository. If possible, use a repository which assigns a DOI and licence.
- Choose an appropriate licence for your materials, code and/or data (see https://creativecommons.org/).
- Always remember version control: give your files a clear name (for both yourself and others!) and include the version number.
- Don't data dump! Make sure you follow the FAIR principles – are your materials, code and data *Findable, Accessible, Interoperable* and *Reusable*?
- If you have a valid reason *not* to share, can you provide a 'README' file that describes your materials, code or data in as much detail as possible for others?
- Include a link or description as to where to find your materials, code and data in any research outputs.
- Remember, 'as open as possible, as closed as necessary'.

(Continued)

⟶

(Continued)

- Cite others' materials, code and data just as you would with a journal article or book (remember, credit where credit is due!).
- Ask for help from your supervisors, colleagues, ethics board or library.

Mistakes in open science and how to avoid them

Throughout this chapter you have learned about many different open science practices that may be new to you. But what you might not realize is that *everyone is a student of open science*, and with learning comes making mistakes. I asked researchers on Twitter and Facebook to let me know about the mistakes they have made in their open science journey so far and also added my own. You can see these in Table 5.4 along with their solutions. I hope this helps to highlight that we are all human – everyone makes mistakes at some point and the most important thing is to implement best practices and correct any errors as you learn. Reinforcing this notion, I highly recommend reading Bartlett's (2017) blog

Table 5.4 Mistakes in open science and how to avoid them

Preprints and open access

Mistake 1: I used to think that open access [OA] meant that I could reuse the material in any way that I wanted. I learned the distinction between the different types of OA by familiarizing myself with Creative Commons licences.
Solution: The respondent identified the solution! Make sure you check the licence attached to the material, code or data and understand the terms for reuse, as well as including appropriate licences for your work. See the guidelines on Creative Commons licensing (https://creativecommons.org/).

Mistake 2: I uploaded my article as a preprint but forgot to check the journal's guidelines for internet posting. I needed to include a brief statement that the preprint had not yet undergone peer review and should be cited with caution.
Solution: Before you post a preprint, check the journal guidelines by visiting their specific website or by using the helpful Sherpa Romeo guidelines (https://v2.sherpa.ac.uk/romeo/). Many journals allow for preprints, and if you simply follow their guidelines you won't go wrong! If you forget to do this or realize you have made this mistake, simply update your preprint to a new version with the relevant statements, or request for the preprint to be removed. As your preprint undergoes the peer review process, update the information in the preprint server: this can include uploading the revised (author) version of your work with the final citation and Digital Object Identifier (DOI). By linking the DOI in the server, citations gathered on the preprint and final publication become merged (happy days!).

Table 5.4   *(Continued)*

Preregistration and Registered Reports

Mistake 1: I did not specify in my preregistration that I was analysing each subscale of a questionnaire, instead writing that I would create an aggregated total from all questionnaire items. It made no sense to look at the total as the questionnaire assessed different theoretical constructs.

Solution: Report this deviation transparently. For example, if your preregistration was via the OSF, you can use their new 'update' feature to make a clear note of this, and if you are using a platform that does not allow for this, you can upload a 'deviations from preregistration' document which outlines any changes and your rationale for them. In the write-up of your report, provide a detailed summary of these and link to your preregistration (with updates) and/or the deviation document.

Mistake 2: I preregistered the incorrect hypotheses (wrong direction!) and an inappropriate statistical test.

Solution: If you spot your mistake before analysis and/or submission/ publication, you can update your preregistration (as above). Be sure to explain why this was incorrect so that the reader/reviewer understands your rationale and can judge this for themselves.

Mistake 3: I didn't explain what I would do with missing data in my preregistration.

Solution: Different preregistration templates ask for different things, so it's easy to miss something like this. You may then come across these problems when discussing or analysing your data. Again, transparently report this in your research report/article. You can also conduct what's known as a 'sensitivity analysis' where you look at, and report, what happens when missing data is analysed in different ways.

Mistake 4: I forgot to preregister a study although I usually do so!

Solution: Transparently report in your report/article that the study was not preregistered. You can follow the American Psychological Association Journal Article Reporting Standards for quantitative, qualitative or mixed-methods designs (https://apastyle.apa.org/jars).

Mistake 5: I thought that I had 'preregistered' my study because I created a folder on my Open Science Framework project page and uploaded a completed template. I did not realize that this would not be classed as a 'true' preregistration.

Solution: This is an easy mistake to make because many preregistration templates can be downloaded from the internet for free and can be saved anywhere you like. However, your preregistration must be uploaded to a verified repository (e.g. https://osf.io/prereg/, https://aspredicted.org) to ensure that it is date/time-stamped, permanent and publicly accessible.

(Continued)

Table 5.4 *(Continued)*

Open materials, code and data

Mistake 1 [open materials]: I uploaded stimulus images to OSF which had author copyright and should not have been shared.
Solution: Check the copyright of stimulus images at the study planning stage to understand sharing and reuse: this is particularly a concern for older materials. Can you use alternative images/materials that can be made open? If not, upload a document ('README' file) onto OSF that explains why the materials can't be shared and transparently report this in your write-up. Share a link to the stimulus set so that researchers can request their access from the original authors.

Mistake 2 [open code]: I uploaded experiment scripts created with licensed software, without realizing that others could not access them if they did not have a licence.
Solution: Many experiment scripts can be exported to text files (.txt), allowing others to at least see the code but not run it. Upload a document that explains how to open as a text file or, even better, upload this yourself so that others can simply download it. Look into open-source experimental software, such as PsychoPy (Peirce et al. 2019).

Mistake 3 [open data]: In the participant consent form, I wrote that data will only be presented at the group level. My intention was for the participants to feel safer when answering the questionnaire, but this made me unable to share all of the data openly (that was not aggregated) despite anonymizing it.
Solution: Get into the habit of including a statement about open data sharing in the participant consent form, and allowing participants to opt in or opt out. In the open data file, you can then share the responses for those who consent and redact the data for those who do not. Alternatively, you can look into simulating the data to have the same statistical properties and allow for reproducibility while maintaining ethical principles (see Quintana 2020). Talk to your ethics committee too, to see if and how data can be shared in instances like these (there are different data protection laws in different countries and sometimes parts of the data can still be shared even without participant consent).

on the mistakes he made during his first preregistration and his learning journey thereafter. We are all in this boat together, but this time around it's floating!

Now you have learned how to embed open science practices in your research workflow you can start to put them into practice, whether that's explaining these to others, using your knowledge in interviews or assessments, or implementing them in your research projects. Remember that you don't have to tick all of these boxes straight away; these skills will take time, and you may want to revisit this chapter a few times and read up on the other recommended resources. This reminds me of a sentiment I heard at the American Psychological Society conference "If you are doing one thing that is open science, you are an open scientist." Take incremental steps to make your science better!

Activity: Ambiguities in study preregistration*

A preregistration should be clear and detailed enough to allow another researcher to understand exactly what is planned and how this will be executed. In other words, it should not be ambiguous. In the examples below I challenge you to (1) identify the ambiguity from a researcher's preregistration, (2) explain why this might be problematic, and (3) provide alternative wording that could improve this. Importantly, make sure that your answer is relevant to the question being asked; for example, if the question theme is 'hypotheses' make sure your answer is based on this rather than another aspect of the study (e.g. 'dependent variable'). I'll start with an example.

Confirmatory analysis:
'For the four levels of memory recall, we will use a one-way ANOVA test on each dependent variable.'

Ambiguity: What are the levels of memory recall? What is each dependent variable? On what measure will this be conducted? How would a significant ANOVA be followed up? Will the researcher assess statistical significance, and what alpha level would be used?

Violation: There is an issue of analytical flexibility: the researcher could plausibly enter any number of levels into the ANOVA because we do not know how many levels there are. Without specifying the precise measure, it is unknown whether the researchers have one or multiple measures of the same construct or are measuring memory recall in multiple ways. This could result in several QRPs, such as selective reporting of the measures that worked, or p-HACKing by running multiple analyses and stopping when $p < .05$.

Alternative: A one-way ANOVA will be conducted with the four levels of memory recall (10 seconds, 20 seconds, 30 seconds, 60 seconds) as the independent variable and the percentage score (out of 100) on the memory recall test as the dependent variable. A significant main effect will be shown by $p < .05$. Any significant effects will be followed up with pairwise comparisons: because there is a possibility of four t-tests being conducted, Bonferroni corrections will be used to correct for multiple comparisons.

Have a go yourself ...

Hypotheses:
'We predict that we will replicate Robinson et al. (2007). In addition, we predict that personality will influence eating behaviour.'

Dependent variables:
'An alcohol questionnaire will be employed to measure participants' self-reported alcohol consumption.'

Confirmatory analyses:
'A 2 by 2 ANOVA will be the designated statistical analysis. This statistical analysis will provide insight into the 2-way interaction.'

* These questions have been adapted from van 't Veer and colleagues (2019) preregistration workshop at APS 2019.

6 | Psychology moving forward

Take a moment to think about the wonderful intricacies of human behaviour that you have learned about through the discipline of psychology. Psychologists have begun to understand the many determinants of mental and physical health, the complex underpinnings of addictive behaviours, the different strategies that can help students to perform better in school, and the development of the human brain from childhood to old age. These are just a handful of examples. Psychological research contributes significantly to the production of knowledge and has transformed our everyday lives: our findings have wide-scale implications and are used in both practice and policy. That is *really, really* cool! However, how do we know which research findings are credible and which are *in*credible? Which findings we can trust and which we should be critical of?

Research is neither perfect nor easy, and it's not meant to be. If it were, we'd have carried out every possible research study and already have the answers to every question. But for research to truly advance human knowledge, it has to be transparent and trustworthy: after all, scientific progress rests on the replicability and reproducibility of the claims it makes. Yet while lots of psychological phenomena successfully replicate (see Klein et al. 2014; Protzko et al. 2020), a recent history of the replication crisis shows that many others crumble under careful re-examination and it is difficult to reproduce previous findings. In this book, I have provided a comprehensive overview of the replication crisis and its many explanations before introducing you to the wave of open science that aims to improve *how* research is conducted, as well as the norms and culture around it. Before I look towards the future with optimism, let's summarize what's been discussed so far.

In Chapter 1, I recounted my experiences studying the phenomenon of stereotype threat during my research degree, and the difficulties I faced when trying to detect reliable effects. I explained how the incentive culture of academia, with its pressure to 'publish or perish' and preoccupation with positive results, impacted my psychological well-being and led me to question a future academic career. I also recalled how I felt on first learning about the replication crisis: a feeling of relief that all of my questions and doubts about my own ability had been answered, followed by an overwhelming sense of dispassion and distrust towards a discipline that I loved. I then reflected on events that would reignite my passion, with the movement of open science fostering deep reflection and ushering in fast-paced improvements to research culture. Not wanting you to go through similar experiences is what motivated me to write this book.

It is my hope that understanding issues in research, and importantly their solutions, will help you to critically engage with psychological science and employ best practices in your own research.

In Chapter 2, I introduced you to the important concepts of replication and reproducibility, distinguishing between exact and conceptual replications and explaining their unique advantages. After describing what science *should* be, I uncovered a series of unfortunate events which plummeted psychology into its recent crisis. I explored John Ioannidis' persuasive publication which exclaimed that 'most published research findings are false', and how researchers have (historically) relied on small, underpowered samples and have fallen prey to flexibility in research design and analysis. Ironically, I then explained how Bem found evidence for precognition across nine experimental studies, followed by the unthinkable: a wide-scale case of academic fraud conducted by Stapel, which caused psychology to worry immensely about its perceived credibility. Then came meta-research, with Simmons et al. (2011) demonstrating how undisclosed flexibility in data analysis could lead to presenting anything as significant, and John et al. (2012) showing how many researchers admitted to exploiting the grey area of research norms by engaging in QRPs. In 2012, Pashler and Wagenmakers declared that psychology was facing a 'crisis of confidence', with empirical findings of this claim following from Many Labs 1 (Klein et al. 2014) and the Open Science Collaboration (2015). Finally, psychologists realized they were not riding the storm alone, with Baker (2016) discussing how researchers from chemistry to medicine to physics found it challenging to replicate or reproduce their own and others' work. At the end of the chapter, I critically examined what a 'failed' replication means, before taking a deeper look at the term 'crisis' and diverse perspectives on whether or not psychology is immersed in one.

Moving on to Chapter 3, I dived 'beneath the iceberg' to explore explanations that underpin replication and reproducibility concerns, centring on a deep-rooted culture of academic incentives, intertwined with various forms of cognitive biases that influence researchers' behaviour and that leak into the publication system. Revisiting QRPs, I defined terms such as *p*-hacking and HARKing, and how these permit us to tell hyped or exaggerated 'stories of research', similar to those on the front covers of magazines. Next, I discussed how the excessive focus on statistical significance in quantitative psychology research can often lead us down the wrong track, before exploring the underappreciated explanation that shaky measures lead to shaky results. Despite the importance of replication in psychology, Chapter 3 also highlighted the virtual absence of replication studies in the literature and detailed how researchers shy away from correcting their mistakes. I ended by explaining how a long history of closed science has generally led to a lack of transparency in the reporting of research.

From pessimism came optimism, and in Chapter 4 I outlined a range of potential solutions for the crisis, subsumed under the umbrella of 'open science'. Here I explained that open science aims to improve research integrity by focusing on accessibility, transparency, rigour, reproducibility and replicability

(Crüwell et al. 2019; Kathawalla et al. 2021), as well as increasing diversity, equity and inclusion (e.g. Ledgerwood et al. 2022). Through implementing practices such as preprints, preregistration, Registered Reports, and open materials, data and code, I showed you how psychology could clean up its act. I then highlighted the potentially transformative power of 'big team science' in accelerating scientific progress, improving researcher and participant diversity, incentivizing replication and avoiding research waste. Along the way, I evaluated some challenges that open science needs to overcome to reach its true potential: ensuring that under-represented voices are welcomed and heard as well as ensuring future-proof, sustained change.

Finally, in Chapter 5, I provided a hands-on guide to implementing different open science practices. Here I showed you how to use the Open Science Framework as a home for all of your open science tools, before outlining steps to implement each of these specifically. I introduced different preprint servers that can enhance the discoverability of your (and others') work and allow you to gain helpful feedback. Next, I guided you through registering a study protocol on a public repository and explained how this can aid research transparency. Levelling up on preregistration, I outlined top tips for writing a Registered Report and explained how this can refocus efforts on designing the most rigorous and high-quality studies without any apprehension associated with the results. Then I dug deeper into open materials, code and data, with a key focus on licensing, copyright, ethics and the FAIR principles. Remember, you don't need to become an expert in all of these practices overnight – take a bite from the open science buffet and keep coming back for more!

In this last chapter, I now want to look towards the future of psychological science, focusing on the potential for open science to reform the replication crisis in psychology (and beyond).

Seeing the replication crisis as an opportunity

When thinking about the term 'crisis', many people focus on its definition as a 'time of intense difficulty' or 'a time when an important decision must be made'. As a result, this term might conjure up negative connotations and, when applied to a research discipline, can lead people to view it pessimistically. However, Hussey (2022) makes the interesting statement that crises are a 'call to action' … 'an urgency that motivates people to act'. With this in mind, the replication crisis can be seen as an opportunity to reflect on which aspects of research practice continue to be effective, what parts can be improved and how this can be sustained to create positive, permanent change (Munafò et al. 2022). Moving forward, it will be important to ensure that each part of the research ecosystem works collaboratively to tackle the challenges, and this includes individuals, institutions, funders and publishers (Stewart et al. 2022). By working together, open and transparent research practices can become routinized and replace age-old research norms. Open science will simply become science *done right*!

Science pursuing and exposing its own flaws is just science being science. Science is trustworthy because it does not trust itself. Science earns that trustworthiness through publicly, transparently, and continuously seeking out and eradicating error in its own culture, methods, and findings. Increasing awareness and evidence of the deleterious effects of reward structures and research practices will spur one of science's greatest strengths, self-correction.

(Errington et al. 2021a: 21)

Why learning about open science is important

Throughout this book, I have discussed the importance of implementing open science in the research process. I have shown you how open science can reduce human biases and shift incentives, aid diverse and equitable collaboration, and enable more reliable, replicable and reproducible research. From the replication crisis comes a credibility revolution, and psychological science can act as a positive role model for other disciplines facing (and still to face) similar challenges. However, there remains a paradox – although conversations about replication concerns and open science are sweeping through the research community, these are arguably lost in the *teaching of psychology*. Robust science requires robust training.

The values of open science are not exclusive to research alone, and for this reason it is essential that they are embedded in teaching (Azevedo et al. 2022). By training the next generation of budding researchers, transparent and inclusive research practices can be continuously passed down. By learning about open science, you will gain skills in research literacy, critical thinking and analytic reasoning, while understanding the value of effective teamwork and transparent communication (Button et al. 2020; Jekel et al. 2020; Pownall et al. 2022). For example, you might start by applying these skills to the evaluation of research, asking yourself: do the authors distinguish clearly between confirmatory and exploratory analyses? Do they use any relevant open science practices, such as preregistration, open materials, data and code, or have they written their article via the Registered Report format? Do they report details clearly enough for you to attempt an independent replication? When developing your own research projects, you may then decide to implement the various open science practices discussed in this book. Perhaps you will initiate a preregistration which can help you to plan a detailed and rigorous research study, understand the value of both significant and non-significant findings, and actively negate Questionable Research Practices (Blincoe and Buchert 2020; Pownall 2020). Or you may want to upload your dissertation or thesis to a public repository so that other people can benefit from reading your work.

There are benefits to engaging with open science beyond this 'good for science' idea too. For those of you who want to pursue a research career, an open science skill set can make you a highly employable graduate! Many research degrees and associated careers recognize the value of open science, and this is becoming an increasingly sought-after skill (Flier 2017). It's also particularly noteworthy that the current fast-paced developments in making psychological science more transparent, accessible, robust and credible are often spearheaded by enthusiastic students and early career researchers, and you can do the same. Even for those of you who pursue a career outside of academia, learning about replication, reproducibility and open science can make you a critical consumer of research. Indeed, research underpins much of our lives; during the COVID-19 pandemic, we saw rapid work being conducted on the efficacy of different vaccines and, more than ever, it was important to be able to critically assess and interpret news sources and scientific findings. Understanding open science can therefore provide you with the necessary tools to promote long-lasting engagement with science (Azevedo et al. 2019; Chopik et al. 2018). Furthermore, these skills can enhance your own writing and communication, digital learning abilities and data management skills (Çetinkaya-Rundel and Ellison 2020; Jarke et al. 2022; Kathawalla et al. 2021). All of these skills are suited to varied careers, such as those in industry, journalism and healthcare, as well as being useful in everyday life.

After reading this book, you may want to find ways to continue your learning about open science, allowing you to keep up to date with evolving initiatives, perceptions and evaluations of these practices, and new questions posed by meta-research. With this in mind, I recommend exploring journal clubs and grassroots initiatives such as *ReproducibiliTEA* and the *RIOT Science Club* (which also share talks on YouTube) and asking about these or similar communities at your university. One way to see publicly available talks is to follow the Open Research Calendar (https://openresearchcalendar.org/calendar/). You can also follow the great work of the *Framework for Open and Reproducible Research Training* (https://forrt.org/), look through the vast array of resources on platforms such as the OSF (https://osf.io/), and follow the work of the different national Reproducibility Networks (e.g. UKRN; https://www.ukrn.org/). Also remember that librarians are valuable people to ask about open science, and lots of interesting discussions can also be found on social media platforms such as Twitter and Mastodon. For the latest articles in meta-research, you can put one open science practice into use immediately by following preprint servers (e.g. MetaArXiv)!

Conclusion

In the name of openness and transparency, I'll tell you a little secret. When the publisher, Open University Press, approached me to write this book, they initially wanted me to provide an overview of the replication crisis. I read the email with excitement as I knew that discussion of replication issues was scarce in teaching and psychology textbooks (particularly social psychology ones). If they don't teach it, then I could!

But I knew that a discussion of replication in psychology had to go well beyond the so-called 'crisis': it had to be about the *opportunities* that open science could bring to repair research culture. I also reflected on my own experiences during my research degree and knew that this could help many other students who experience the same challenges or feel the way that I felt. Yet with anything new, it can feel overwhelming and daunting to learn about different practices or know when and how to implement them, and so I knew I had to provide a handy guide too. I hope that this book achieves its goals by providing an accessible overview of the replication crisis and a helpful guide for understanding and implementing open science practices. As psychology moves forward into the era of open science, many new terms will emerge, innovative initiatives will evolve and meta-research will teach which practices work best. I therefore want to leave you with this reminder: **we are *all* students of open science, and we will be for many years to come!**

References

Abdill, R.J. and Blekman, R. (2019). Meta-research: Tracking the popularity and outcomes of all bioRxiv preprints, *eLife*, 8: 245133. Available at https://doi.org/10.7554/eLife.45133 (accessed 31 August 2022).

Adams, R.C., Button, K.S., Hickey, L. et al. (2021). Food-related inhibitory control training reduces food liking but not snacking frequency or weight in a large healthy adult sample, *Appetite*, 167: 105601. Available at https://doi.org/10.1016/j.appet.2021.105601 (accessed 31 August 2022).

Adewumi, M.T., Vo, N., Tritz, D., Beaman, J. and Vassar, M. (2021). An evaluation of the practice of transparency and reproducibility in addiction medicine literature, *Addictive Behaviors*, 112: 106560. Available at https://doi.org/10.1016/j.addbeh.2020.106560 (accessed 31 August 2022).

Allen, C. and Mehler, D.M.A. (2019). Open science challenges, benefits and tips in early career and beyond, *PLoS Biology*, 17: e3000587. Available at https://doi.org/10.1371/journal.pbio.3000587 (accessed 31 August 2022).

Altschul, D.M., Beran, M.J., Bohn, M. et al. (2019). Establishing an infrastructure for collaboration in primate cognition research, *PLoS One*, 14: e0223675. Available at http://dx.doi.org/10.1371/journal.pone.0223675 (accessed 31 August 2022).

American Psychological Association (APA) (2002). Ethical principles of psychologists and code of conduct, American Psychological Association website. Available at https://www.apa.org/ethics/code/ethics-code-2017.pdf (accessed 31 August 2022).

Anderson, C.J., Bahník, Š., Barnett-Cowan, M. et al. (2016). Response to comment on 'estimating the reproducibility of psychological science', *Science*, 351: 1037. Available at https://doi.org/10.1126/science.aad9163 (accessed 31 August 2022).

Antonakis, J. (2017). On doing better science: From thrill of discovery to policy implications, *Leadership Quarterly*, 28: 5–21. Available at https://doi.org/10.1016/j.leaqua.2017.01.006 (accessed 31 August 2022).

Armeni, K., Brinkman, L., Carlsson, R. et al. (2021). Towards wide-scale adoption of open science practices: The role of open science communities, *Science & Public Policy*, 48: 605–11. Available at https://doi.org/10.1093/scipol/scab039 (accessed 31 August 2022).

Azevedo, F., Liu, M., Pennington, C.R. et al. (2022). Towards a culture of open scholarship: The role of pedagogical communities, *BMC Research Notes*, 15: 1–5. Available at https://doi.org/10.1186/s13104-022-05944-1 (accessed 31 August 2022).

Azevedo, F., Parsons, S., Micheli, L. et al. (2019). Introducing a Framework for Open and Reproducible Research Training (FORRT), *OSF Preprints*, 13 December. Available at https://doi.org/10.31219/osf.io/bnh7p (accessed 31 August 2022).

Baker, M. (2016). 1,500 scientists lift the lid on reproducibility, *Nature*, 533: 452–4. Available at https://doi.org/10.1038/533452a (accessed 31 August 2022).

Bakker, M., Veldkamp, C.L.S., van Assen, M.A.L.M. et al. (2020). Ensuring the quality and specificity of preregistrations, *PLoS Biology*, 18: e3000937. Available at https://doi.org/10.1371/journal.pbio.3000937 (accessed 31 August 2022).

Barber, S.J., Mather, M. and Gatz, M. (2015). How stereotype threat affects healthy older adults' performance on clinical assessments of cognitive decline: The key role of regulatory fit, *The Journals of Gerontology: Series B*, 70: 891–900. Available at https://doi.org/10.1093/geronb/gbv009 (accessed 31 August 2022).

Bartlett, J. (2017). How to effectively pre-register your research: A case-study of my own mistakes. *James E. Bartlett* [online blog], 29 March. Available at https://bartlettje. github.io/2017-03-29-effective-preregistration/ (accessed 31 August 2022).

Bartlett, J. (2020). Sharing research materials online: Why you should and how you can, *Gorilla*™ [online blog]. Available at https://gorilla.sc/sharing-research-materials-on-line-why-you-should-and-how-you-can/ (accessed 31 August 2022).

Bartlett, J. and Eaves, J. (2019). Getting to grips with open science, in H. Walton (ed.), *Guide for Psychology Postgraduates: Surviving Postgraduate Study*, 2nd edn. British Psychological Society, pp. 85–9. Available at https://osf.io/b68qd/ (accessed 31 August 2022).

Baumeister, R.F., Bratslavsky, E., Muraven, M. and Tice, D.M. (1998). Ego depletion: Is the active self a limited resource?, *Journal of Personality & Social Psychology*, 74: 1252–65. Available at https://doi.org/10.1037/0022-3514.74.5.1252 (accessed 31 August 2022).

Begley, C.G. and Ellis, L.M. (2012). Raise standards for preclinical cancer research, *Nature*, 483: 531–3. Available at https://doi.org/10.1038/483531a (accessed 31 August 2022).

Beilock, S.L., Jellison, W.A., Rydell, R.J., McConnell, A.R. and Carr, T.H. (2006). On the causal mechanisms of stereotype threat: Can skills that don't rely heavily on working memory still be threatened?, *Personality & Social Psychology Bulletin*, 32: 1059–71. Available at https://doi.org/10.1177/0146167206288489 (accessed 31 August 2022).

Beilock, S.L. and McConnell, A.R. (2004). Stereotype threat and sport: Can athletic performance be threatened?, *Journal of Sport & Exercise Psychology*, 26: 597–609. Available at https://doi.org/10.1123/jsep.26.4.597 (accessed 31 August 2022).

Belluz, J. (2015). Scientists often fail when they try to replicate studies. This psychologist explains why, *Vox*, 27 August. Available at https://www.vox.com/2015/8/27/9212161/psychology-replication (accessed 31 August 2022).

Bem, D.J. (2011). Feeling the future: Experimental evidence for anomalous retroactive influences on cognition and affect, *Journal of Personality & Social Psychology*, 100: 407–25. Available at https://doi.org/10.1037/a0021524 (accessed 31 August 2022).

Benjamin, D.J., Berger, J.O., Johannesson, M. et al. (2018). Redefine statistical significance, *Nature Human Behavior*, 2: 6–10. Available at https://doi.org/10.1038/s41562-017-0189-z (accessed 31 August 2022).

Bergmann, C. (2018). How to integrate open science into language acquisition research. Student workshop at the 43rd Boston University Conference on Language Development (BUCLD), Boston, USA. Available at https://docs.google.com/presentation/d/1bdICPzPOFs7V5aOZA2OdQgSAvgoB6WQweI21kVpk9Gg/edit#slide=id.p (accessed 31 August 2022).

Besançon, L., Peiffer-Smadja, N., Segalas, C. et al. (2021). Open science saves lives: Lessons from the COVID-19 pandemic, *BMC Medical Research Methodology*, 21: 1–18. Available at https://doi.org/10.1186/s12874-021-01304-y (accessed 31 August 2022).

Beyer, F., Flannery, J., Gau, R. et al. (2021). A fMRI pre-registration template, *PsychArchives*. Available at https://doi.org/10.23668/PSYCHARCHIVES.5121 (accessed 31 August 2022).

Bik, E.M., Fang, F.C., Kullas, A.L., Davis, R.J. and Casadevall, A. (2018). Analysis and correction of inappropriate image duplication: The *Molecular and Cellular Biology* Experience, *Molecular and Cell Biology*, 38: e00309–18. Available at https://doi.org/10.1128/MCB.00309-18 (accessed 31 August 2022).

Bishop, D. (2018). Fallibility in science: Responding to errors in the work of oneself and others, *Advances in Methods & Practices in Psychological Science*, 1: 432–8. Available at https://doi.org/10.1177%2F2515245918776632 (accessed 31 August 2022).

Blincoe, S. and Buchert, S. (2020). Research preregistration as a teaching and learning tool in undergraduate psychology courses, *Psychology Learning & Teaching*, 19: 107–15. Available at https://doi.org/10.1177/1475725719875844 (accessed 31 August 2022).

Boekel, W., Wagenmakers, E.-J., Belay, L. et al. (2015). A purely confirmatory replication study of structural brain–behavior correlations, *Cortex*, 66: 115–33. Available at https://doi.org/10.1016/j.cortex.2014.11.019 (accessed 31 August 2022).

Bosnjak, M., Fiebach, C.J., Mellor, D. et al. (2022). A template for preregistration of quantitative research in psychology: Report of the joint psychological societies preregistration task force, *American Psychologist*, 77: 602–15. Available at https://doi.org/10.1037/amp0000879 (accessed 31 August 2022).

Botvinik-Nezer, R., Holzmeister, F., Camerer, C.F. et al. (2020). Variability in the analysis of a single neuroimaging dataset by many teams, *Nature*, 582: 84–8. Available at https://doi.org/10.1038/s41586-020-2314-9 (accessed 31 August 2022).

Bourne, P.E., Polka, J.K., Vale, R.D. and Kiley, R. (2017). Ten simple rules to consider regarding preprint submission, *PLoS Computer Biology*, 13: 1005473. Available at https://doi.org/10.1371/journal.pcbi.1005473 (accessed 31 August 2022).

Bowman, S.D., DeHaven, A.C., Errington, T.M. et al. (2020). OSF Prereg Template, *Meta-ArXiv*, 22 January. Available at https://doi.org/10.31222/osf.io/epgjd (accessed 31 August 2022).

Brandt, M.J., IJzerman, H., Dijksterhuis, A. et al. (2014). The Replication Recipe: What makes for a convincing replication?, *Journal of Experimental Social Psychology*, 50: 217–24. Available at https://doi.org/10.1016/j.jesp.2013.10.005 (accessed 31 August 2022).

Branney, P., Reid, K., Frost, N. et al. (2019). A context-consent meta-framework for designing open (qualitative) data studies, *Qualitative Research in Psychology*, 16: 483–502. Available at https://doi.org/10.1080/14780887.2019.1605477 (accessed 31 August 2022).

British Psychological Society (2019). *Standards for the Accreditation of Undergraduate, Conversion and Integrated Masters Programmes in Psychology*. British Psychological Society. Available at https://cms.bps.org.uk/sites/default/files/2022-07/Undergraduate%20Accreditation%20Handbook%202019.pdf (accessed 31 August 2022).

British Psychological Society (2021). *BPS Code of Human Research Ethics*. British Psychological Society.

Butler, N., Delaney, H. and Spoelstra, S. (2017). The gray zone: Questionable research practices in the business school, *Academy of Management Learning & Education*, 16: 94–109. Available at http://dx.doi.org/10.5465/amle.2015.0201 (accessed 31 August 2022).

Button, K.S., Chambers, C.D., Lawrence, N. and Munafò, M.R. (2020). Grassroots training for reproducible science: A consortium-based approach to the empirical dissertation, *Psychology, Learning & Teaching*, 19: 77–90. Available at https://doi.org/10.1177/1475725719857659 (accessed 31 August 2022).

Button, K.S., Ioannidis, J.P.A., Mokrysz, C. et al. (2013). Power failure: Why small sample size undermines the reliability of neuroscience, *Nature Reviews Neuroscience*, 14: 365–76. Available at https://doi.org/10.1038/nrn3475 (accessed 31 August 2022).

Button, K.S., Lawrence, N.S., Chambers, C.D. and Munafò, M.R. (2016). Instilling scientific rigour at the grassroots, *The Psychologist*, 29: 158–9.

Camerer, C.F., Dreber, A., Forsell, E. et al. (2016). Evaluating replicability of laboratory experiments in economics, *Science*, 351: 1433–6. Available at https://doi.org/10.1126/science.aaf0918 (accessed 31 August 2022).

Campbell, M., Katikireddi, S.V., Sowden, A. and Thomson, H. (2019). Lack of transparency in reporting narrative synthesis of quantitative data: A methodological assessment of systematic reviews, *Journal of Clinical Epidemiology*, 105: 1–9. Available at https://doi.org/10.1016/j.jclinepi.2018.08.019 (accessed 31 August 2022).

Carter, T.J., Ferguson, M.J. and Hassin, R.R. (2011). A single exposure to the American flag shifts support toward Republicanism up to 8 months later, *Psychological Science*, 22: 1011–18. Available at https://doi.org/10.1177%2F0956797611414726 (accessed 31 August 2022).

Caruso, E.M., Vohs, K.D., Baxter, B. and Waytz, A. (2013). Mere exposure to money increases endorsement of free-market systems and social inequality, *Journal of Experimental Psychology: General*, 142: 301–6. Available at https://doi.org/10.1037/a0029288 (accessed 31 August 2022).

Çetinkaya-Rundel, M. and Ellison, V. (2020). A fresh look at introductory data science, *Journal of Statistics & Data Science Education*, 29: S16–S26. Available at https://doi.org/10.1080/10691898.2020.1804497 (accessed 31 August 2022).

Chambers, C.D. (2013). Registered Reports: A new publishing initiative at Cortex [Editorial], *Cortex*, 49: 609–10. Available at https://doi.org/10.1016/j.cortex.2012.12.016 (accessed 31 August 2022).

Chambers, C.D. and Tzavella, L. (2021). The past, present and future of Registered Reports, *Nature Human Behaviour*, 6: 29–42. Available at https://doi.org/10.1038/s41562-021-01193-7 (accessed 31 August 2022).

Chang, A.C. and Li, P. (2015). Is economics research replicable? Sixty published papers from thirteen journals say 'usually not'. FEDS Working Paper No. 2015-083. Available at http://dx.doi.org/10.17016/FEDS.2015.083 (accessed 31 August 2022).

Chang, A.C. and Li, P. (2022). Is economics research replicable? Sixty published papers from thirteen journals say 'often not', *Critical Finance Review*, 11. Available at http://dx.doi.org/10.1561/104.00000053 (accessed 31 August 2022).

Chartier, C.R., Riegelman, A. and McCarthy, R.J. (2018). StudySwap: A platform for interlab replication, collaboration, and resource exchange, *Advances in Methods & Practices in Psychological Science*, 1: 574–9. Available at https://doi.org/10.1177%2F2515245918808767 (accessed 31 August 2022).

Chopik, W.J., Bremner, R.H., Defever, A.M. and Keller, V.N. (2018). How (and whether) to teach undergraduates about the replication crisis in psychological science, *Teaching of Psychology*, 45: 158–63. Available at https://doi.org/10.1177%2F0098628318762900 (accessed 31 August 2022).

Claesen, A., Gomes, S., Tuerlinckx, F. and Vanpaemel, W. (2021). Comparing dream to reality: An assessment of adherence of the first generation of preregistered studies, *Royal Society Open Science*, 8: 211037. Available at https://doi.org/10.1098/rsos.211037 (accessed 31 August 2022).

Cobb, M. (2017). The prehistory of biology preprints: A forgotten experiment from the 1960s, *PLoS Biology*, 15: e2003995. Available at https://doi.org/10.1371/journal.pbio.2003995 (accessed 31 August 2022).

Cohen, J. (1988). *Statistical Power Analysis for the Behavioral Sciences*, 2nd edn. Lawrence Erlbaum Associates.

Colavizza, G., Hrynaszkiewicz, I., Staden, I., Whitaker, K. and McGillivray, B. (2020). The citation advantage of linking publications to research data, *PLoS One*, 15: e0230416. Available at https://doi.org/10.1371/journal.pone.0230416 (accessed 31 August 2022).

Coles, N.A., March, D.S., Marmolejo-Ramos, F. et al. (2022). A multi-lab test of the facial feedback hypothesis by the Many Smiles Collaboration. *Nature Human Behaviour*. Available at https://doi.org/10.1038/s41562-022-01458-9

Coles, N.A., Tiokhin, L., Scheel, A.M., Isager, P.M. and Lakens, D. (2018). The costs and benefits of replication studies, *Behaviour & Brain Sciences*, 41: e124. Available at https://doi.org/doi:10.1017/S0140525X18000596 (accessed 31 August 2022).

Colling, L.J. and Szűcs, D. (2021). Statistical inference and the replication crisis, *Review of Philosophy & Psychology*, 12: 121–47. Available at https://doi.org/10.1007/s13164-018-0421-4 (accessed 31 August 2022).

Cook, T.D. and Campbell, D.T. (1979). *Quasi-Experimentation: Design and Analysis Issues for Field Settings*. Houghton Mifflin Company.

Corker, K. (2018). Open science is a behavior, Center for Open Science website, 12 September. Available at https://cos.io/blog/open-science-is-a-behavior/ (accessed 31 August 2022).

Cova, F., Strickland, B., Abatista, A. et al. (2021). Estimating the reproducibility of experimental philosophy, *Review of Philosophy & Psychology*, 12: 9–44. Available at https://doi.org/10.1007/s13164-018-0400-9 (accessed 31 August 2022).

Cronbach, L.J. and Meehl, P.E. (1955). Construct validity in psychological tests, *Psychological Bulletin*, 52: 281–302. Available at https://psycnet.apa.org/doi/10.1037/h0040957 (accessed 31 August 2022).

Crüwell, S. and Evans, N.J. (2021). Preregistration in diverse contexts: A preregistration template for the application of cognitive models, *Royal Society Open Science*, 8: 210155. Available at https://doi.org/10.1098/rsos.210155 (accessed 31 August 2022).

Crüwell, S., van Doorn, J., Etz, A. et al. (2019). Seven easy steps to open science: An annotated reading list, *Zeitschrift für Psychologie*, 227: 237–48. Available at https://doi.org/10.1027/2151-2604/a000387 (accessed 31 August 2022).

Cumming, G. (2011). *Understanding the New Statistics: Effect Sizes, Confidence Intervals, and Meta-Analysis*. Routledge.

Cumming, G. (2013). The new statistics: Why and how, *Psychological Science*, 25: 7–29. Available at https://doi.org/10.1177%2F0956797613504966 (accessed 31 August 2022).

Cumming, G., Fidler, F., Kalinowski, P. and Lai, J. (2012). The statistical recommendations of the American Psychological Association Publication Manual: Effect sizes, confidence intervals, and meta-analysis, *Australian Journal of Psychology*, 64: 138–46. Available at https://doi.org/10.1111/j.1742-9536.2011.00037.x (accessed 31 August 2022).

Dang, J., Barker, P., Baumert, A. et al. (2021). A multilab replication of the ego depletion effect, *Social Psychological & Personality Science*, 12: 14–24. Available at https://doi.org/10.1177%2F1948550619887702 (accessed 31 August 2022).

de Vries, Y., Roest, A.M., de Jonge, P., Cuijpers, P., Munafò, M.R. and Bastiaansen, J.A. (2018). The cumulative effect of reporting and citation biases on the apparent efficacy of treatments: The case of depression, *Psychological Medicine*, 48: 1–3. Available at https://doi.org/10.1017/S0033291718001873 (accessed 31 August 2022).

DeHaven, A. (2017). Preregistration: A plan, not a prison, Center for Open Science website, 23 May. Available at https://www.cos.io/blog/preregistration-plan-not-prison#:~:text=Preregistration%20is%20the%20process%20of,decisions%20before%20conducting%20the%20experiment.&text=As%20you'll%20see%2C%20this,made%20to%20the%20planned%20research (accessed 31 August 2022).

Dennis, A.R. and Valacich, J.S. (2015). A replication manifesto, *AIS Transactions on Replication Research*, 1: 1–4. Available at https://doi.org/10.17705/1atrr.00001 (accessed 31 August 2022).

Descôteaux, J. (2007). Statistical power: An historical introduction, *Tutorials in Quantitative Methods for Psychology*, 3: 28–34. Available at https://doi.org/10.20982/tqmp.03.2.p028 (accessed 31 August 2022).

Dickersin, K. (1990). The existence of publication bias and risk factors for its occurrence, *Journal of the American Medical Association*, 263: 1385–9. Available at https://doi.org/10.1001/jama.1990.03440100097014 (accessed 31 August 2022).

Dunlap, K. (1926). The experimental methods of psychology, in C. Murchison (ed.) *Psychologies of 1925*. Clark University Press, pp. 331–53. Available at https://psycnet.apa.org/doi/10.1037/11020-000 (accessed 31 August 2022).

Easterbrook, S. (2014). Open code for open science?, *Nature Geoscience*, 7: 779–81. Available at https://doi.org/10.1038/ngeo2283 (accessed 31 August 2022).

Ebersole, C.R., Atherton, O.E., Belanger, A.L. et al. (2016a). Many Labs 3: Evaluating participant pool quality across the academic semester via replication, *Journal of Experimental Social Psychology*, 67: 68–82. Available at https://doi.org/10.1016/j.jesp.2015.10.012 (accessed 31 August 2022).

Ebersole, C.R., Axt, J.R. and Nosek, B.A. (2016b). Scientists' reputations are based on getting it right, not being right, *PLoS Biology*, 14: e1002460. Available at https://doi.org/10.1371/journal.pbio.1002460 (accessed 31 August 2022).

Ebersole, C.R., Mathur, M.B., Baranski, E. et al. (2020). Many Labs 5: Testing pre-data-collection peer review as an intervention to increase replicability, *Advances in Methods & Practices in Psychological Science*, 3: 309–31. Available at https://doi.org/10.1177%2F2515245920958687 (accessed 31 August 2022).

Edwards, M.A. and Roy, S. (2016). Academic research in the 21st century: Maintaining scientific integrity in a climate of perverse incentives and hypercompetition, *Environmental Engineering Science*, 34: 51–61. Available at https://doi.org/10.1089/ees.2016.0223 (accessed 31 August 2022).

Eich, E. (2013). PSCI initiatives for 2013 [uploaded by Brian Nosek as a letter from the Editor of *Psychological Science*]. *Google Groups*. Available at https://groups.google.com/g/opensscienceframework/c/OUYVC0CqU6Y (accessed 31 August 2022).

Engber, D. (2017). Daryl Bem proved ESP is real, which means science is broken, *Slate*, 7 June. Available at https://slate.com/health-and-science/2017/06/daryl-bem-proved-esp-is-real-showed-science-is-broken.html (accessed 31 August 2022).

Errington, T.M., Denis, A., Perfito, N., Iorns, E. and Nosek, B.A. (2021b). Reproducibility in cancer biology: Challenges for assessing replicability in preclinical cancer biology, *eLife*, 10: e67995. Available at https://doi.org/10.7554/eLife.67995 (accessed 31 August 2022).

Errington, T.M., Mathur, M., Soderberg, C.K. et al. (2021a). Investigating the replicability of preclinical cancer biology, *eLife*, 10: e71601. Available at https://doi.org/10.7554/eLife.71601 (accessed 31 August 2022).

European Commission (2016). *H2020 Programme: Guidelines on FAIR Data Management in Horizon 2020*. Version 3.0, 26 July. EC Directorate-General for Research & Innovation. Available at https://ec.europa.eu/research/participants/data/ref/h2020/grants_manual/hi/oa_pilot/h2020-hi-oa-data-mgt_en.pdf (accessed 31 August 2022).

European University Association (2022). *The EUA Open Science Agenda 2025*. European University Association. Available at https://eua.eu/component/attachments/attachments.html?id=3497 (accessed 31 August 2022).

Fabrigar, L.R., Wegener, D.T. and Petter, R.E. (2020). A validity-based framework for understanding replication in psychology, *Personality & Social Psychology Review*, 24: 316–44. Available at https://doi.org/10.1177%2F1088868320931366 (accessed 31 August 2022).

Fanelli, D. (2010). 'Positive' results increase down the hierarchy of the sciences, *PLoS One*, 5: e10068. Available at https://doi.org/10.1371/journal.pone.0010068 (accessed 31 August 2022).

Fanelli, D. (2018). Opinion: Is science really facing a reproducibility crisis, and do we need it to?, *Proceedings of the National Academy of Sciences of the United States of America*, 115: 2628–31. Available at https://doi.org/10.1073/pnas.1708272114 (accessed 31 August 2022).

Ferguson, C.J. and Heene, M. (2012). A vast graveyard of undead theories: Publication bias and psychological science's aversion to the null, *Perspectives on Psychological Science*, 7: 555–61. Available at https://doi.org/10.1177%2F1745691612459059 (accessed 31 August 2022).

Feynman, R.P. (1974). Cargo cult science, *Engineering and Science*, 37: 10–13.

Field, S. (2020). On the beauty of publishing an ugly Registered Report, *Bayesian Spectacles*, 9 April. Available at https://www.bayesianspectacles.org/on-the-beauty-of-publishing-an-ugly-registered-report/ (accessed 31 August 2022).

Field, S.M., Hoeksra, R., Bringmann, L. and van Ravenzwaaij, D. (2019). When and why to replicate: As easy as 1, 2, 3?, *Collabra: Psychology*, 5: 46. Available at https://doi.org/10.1525/collabra.218 (accessed 31 August 2022).

Fink, A. (2010). Survey research methods, *International Encyclopedia of Education*, 3rd edn. Elsevier. Available at https://doi.org/10.1016/B978-0-08-044894-7.00296-7 (accessed 31 August 2022).

Finnigan, K.M. and Corker, K.S. (2016). Do performance avoidance goals moderate the effect of different types of stereotype threat on women's math performance?, *Journal of Research in Personality*, 63: 36–43. Available at https://doi.org/10.1016/j.jrp.2016.05.009 (accessed 31 August 2022).

Firestein, S. (2012). *Ignorance: How It Drives Science*. Oxford University Press.

Fisher, R.A. (1934). *Statistical Methods for Research Workers*, 5th edn. Oliver and Boyd.

Fisher, R.A. (1955). Statistical methods and scientific induction, *Journal of the Royal Statistical Society, Series B*, 17: 69–78. Available at https://doi.org/10.1111/j.2517-6161.1955.tb00180.x (accessed 31 August 2022).

Flake, J.K. and Fried, E.I. (2020). Measurement schmeasurement: Questionable measurement practices and how to avoid them, *Advances in Methods & Practices in Psychological Science*, 3: 456–65. Available at https://doi.org/10.1177%2F2515245920952393 (accessed 31 August 2022).

Flake, J., Pek, J. and Hehman, E. (2017). Construct validation in social and personality research: Current practice and recommendations, *Social Psychological & Personality Science*, 8: 370–8. Available at https://doi.org/10.1177%2F1948550617693063 (accessed 31 August 2022).

Flier, J. (2017). Faculty promotion must assess reproducibility, *Nature*, 549: 133. Available at https://doi.org/10.1038/549133a (accessed 31 August 2022).

Flore, P.C., Mulder, J. and Wicherts, J.M. (2018). The influence of gender stereotype threat on mathematics test scores of Dutch high school students: A Registered Report, *Comprehensive Results in Social Psychology*, 3: 140–74. Available at https://doi.org/10.1080/23743603.2018.1559647 (accessed 31 August 2022).

Forscher, P.S., Wagenmakers, E., Coles, N.A. et al. (2022). The benefits, barriers, and risks of big team science, *Perspectives on Psychological Science*, 1–17. Available at https://doi.org/10.1177/17456916221082970

Foster, E.D. and Deardorff, A. (2017). Open Science Framework (OSF), *Journal of the Medical Library Association*, 105: 203–6. Available at https://dx.doi.org/10.5195%2Fjmla.2017.88 (accessed 31 August 2022).

Franco, A., Malhotra, N. and Simonovits, G. (2014). Publication bias in the social sciences: Unlocking the file drawer, *Science*, 345: 6203. Available at https://doi.org/10.1126/science.1255484 (accessed 31 August 2022).

Frank, M.C., Alcock, K.J., Arias-Trejo, N. et al. (2020). Quantifying sources of variability in infancy research using the infant-directed-speech preference, *Advances in Methods & Practices in Psychological Science*, 3: 24–52. Available at http://dx.doi.org/10.1177/2515245919900809 (accessed 31 August 2022).

Freedman, L.P., Cockburn, I.M. and Simcoe, T.S. (2015). The economics of reproducibility in preclinical research, *PLoS Biology*, 13: e1002165. Available at https://dx.doi.org/10.1371%2Fjournal.pbio.1002165 (accessed 31 August 2022).

Friese, M. and Frankenbach, J. (2020). P-hacking and publication bias interact to distort meta-analytic effect size estimates, *Psychological Methods*, 25: 456–71. Available at https://doi.org/10.1037/met0000246 (accessed 31 August 2022).

Frith, U. (2020). Fast lane to slow science, *Trends in Cognitive Sciences*, 24: 1–2. Available at https://doi.org/10.1016/j.tics.2019.10.007 (accessed 31 August 2022).

Fu, D.Y. and Hughey, J.J. (2019). Meta-research: Releasing a preprint is associated with more attention and citations for the peer-reviewed article, *eLife*, 8: e53646. Available at https://doi.org/10.7554/eLife.52646 (accessed 31 August 2022).

Fyfe, E.R., de Leeuw, J.R., Carvalho, P.F. et al. (2021). Many Classes 1: Assessing the generalizable effect of immediate feedback versus delayed feedback across many college classes, *Advances in Methods & Practices in Psychological Science*, 4: 1–24. Available at https://doi.org/10.1177%2F25152459211027575 (accessed 31 August 2022).

Galak, J., LeBoeuf, R.A., Nelson, L.D. and Simmons, J.P. (2012). Correcting the past: Failures to replicate ψ, *Journal of Personality & Social Psychology*, 103: 933–48. Available at https://psycnet.apa.org/doi/10.1037/a0029709 (accessed 31 August 2022).

Gelman, A. and Loken, E. (2014). The statistical crisis in science, *American Scientist*, 102: 460–5. Available at https://www.americanscientist.org/article/the-statistical-crisis-in-science (accessed 31 August 2022).

Ghelfi, E., Christopherson, C.D., Urry, H.L. et al. (2020). Reexamining the effect of gustatory disgust on moral judgment: A multilab direct replication of Eskine, Kacinik, and Prinz (2011), *Advances in Methods & Practices in Psychological Science*, 3: 3–23. Available at https://doi.org/10.1177%2F2515245919881152 (accessed 31 August 2022).

Gibson, C.E., Losee, J. and Vitiello, C. (2014). A replication attempt of stereotype susceptibility (Shih, Pittinsky, and Ambady, 1999): Identity salience and shifts in quantitative performance, *Social Psychology*, 45: 194–8. Available at https://doi.org/10.1027/1864-9335/a000184 (accessed 31 August 2022).

Gilbert, D.T., King, G., Pettigrew, S. and Wilson, T.D. (2016). Comment on 'estimating the reproducibility of psychological science', *Science*, 351: 1037. Available at https://doi.org/10.1126/science.aad7243 (accessed 31 August 2022).

Gilmore, R.O., Kennedy, J.L. and Adolph, K.E. (2018). Practical solutions for sharing data and materials from psychological research, *Advances in Methods & Practices in Psychological Science*, 1: 121–30. Available at https://doi.org/10.1177/2515245917746500 (accessed 31 August 2022).

Giner-Sorolla, R. (2012). Science or art? How aesthetic standards grease the way through the publication bottleneck but undermine science, *Perspectives on Psychological Science*, 7: 562–71. Available at https://doi.org/10.1177/1745691612457576 (accessed 31 August 2022).

Goldacre, B., Drysdale, H., Dale, A. et al. (2019). COMPare: A prospective cohort study correcting and monitoring 58 misreported trials in real time, *Trials*, 20: 1–16. Available at https://doi.org/10.1186/s13063-019-3173-2 (accessed 31 August 2022).

Grady, D.G., Cummings, S.R. and Hulley, S.B. (2013). Research using existing data, in S.B. Hulley, S.R. Cummings, W.S. Browner, D.G. Grady and T.B. Newman (eds) *Designing Clinical Research*. Lippincott Williams & Wilkins, pp. 192–204.

Grahe, J. (2015). Another step towards scientific transparency: Requiring research materials for publication, *Journal of Social Psychology*, 158: 1–6. Available at https://doi.org/10.1080/00224545.2018.1416272 (accessed 31 August 2022).

Grand, J.A., Rogelberg, S.G., Banks, G.C., Landis, R.S. and Tonidandel, S. (2018). From outcome to process focus: Fostering a more robust psychological science through Registered Reports and results-blind reviewing, *Perspectives on Psychological Science*, 13: 448–56. Available at https://doi.org/10.1177/1745691618767883 (accessed 31 August 2022).

Greenwald, A.G. (1975). Consequences of prejudice against the null hypothesis, *Psychological Bulletin*, 82: 1–20. Available at https://doi.org/10.1037/h0076157 (accessed 31 August 2022).

Griggs, R.A. and Whitehead, G.I. (2014). Coverage of the Stanford prison experiment in introductory social psychology textbooks, *Teaching of Psychology*, 41: 318–24. Available at https://doi.org/10.1177/0098628314549703 (accessed 31 August 2022).

Griggs, R.A. and Whitehead, G.I. (2015). Coverage of Milgram's obedience experiments in social psychology textbooks: Where have all the criticisms gone?, *Teaching of Psychology*, 42: 315–22. Available at https://doi.org/10.1177%2F0098628315603065 (accessed 31 August 2022).

Hagger, M.S., Chatzisarantis, N.L., Alberts, H. et al. (2016). A multi-lab preregistered replication of the ego-depletion effect, *Perspectives on Psychological Science*, 11: 546–73. Available at https://doi.org/10.1177%2F1745691616652873 (accessed 31 August 2022).

Hagger, M.S., Wood, C., Stiff, C. and Chatzisarantis, N.L.D. (2010). Ego depletion and the strength model of self-control: A meta-analysis, *Psychological Bulletin*, 136: 495–525. Available at https://doi.org/10.1037/a0019486 (accessed 31 August 2022).

Hardwicke, T.E. and Ioannidis, J.P.A. (2018). Mapping the universe of registered reports, *Nature Human Behaviour*, 2: 793–6. Available at https://doi.org/10.1038/s41562-018-0444-y (accessed 31 August 2022).

Hardwicke, T.E., Mathur, M.B., MacDonald, K. et al. (2018). Data availability, reusability, and analytic reproducibility: Evaluating the impact of a mandatory open data policy at the journal *Cognition*, *Royal Society Open Science*, 5: 180448. Available at https://doi.org/10.1098/rsos.180448 (accessed 31 August 2022).

Hardwicke, T.E., Serghiou, S., Janiaud, P. et al. (2020). Calibrating the scientific ecosystem through meta-research, *Annual Review of Statistics and Its Application*, 7: 11–37. Available at https://doi.org/10.1146/annurev-statistics-031219-041104 (accessed 31 August 2022).

Hardwicke, T.E., Szűcs, D., Thibault, R.T. et al. (2021). Citation patterns following a strongly contradictory replication result: Four case studies from psychology, *Advances in Methods & Practices in Psychological Science*, 4: 1–14. Available at https://doi.org/10.1177/25152459211040837 (accessed 31 August 2022).

Hardwicke, T.E., Thibault, R.T., Kosie, J.E., Wallach, J.D., Kidwell, M.C. and Ioannidis, J.P. (2022). Estimating the prevalence of transparency and reproducibility-related research practices in psychology (2014–2017), *Perspectives on Psychological Science*, 17: 239–51. Available at https://doi.org/10.1177/1745691620979806 (accessed 31 August 2022).

Hardwicke, T.E. and Wagenmakers, E.-J. (2021). Preregistration: A pragmatic tool to increase transparency, reduce bias, and calibrate confidence in scientific research, *MetaArXiv*, 23 April. Available at https://osf.io/preprints/metaarxiv/d7bcu/download (accessed 31 August 2022).

Haroz, S. (2022). Comparison of Preregistration Platforms, *MetaArXiv*, 24 February. Available at https://doi.org/10.31222/osf.io/zry2u (accessed 31 August 2022).

Haven, T.L., Errington, T.M., Skrede Gleditsch, K. et al. (2020). Preregistering qualitative research: A Delphi study, *International Journal of Qualitative Methods*, 19: 1–13. Available at https://doi.org/10.1177/1609406920976417 (accessed 31 August 2022).

Haven, T.L. and van Grootel, L. (2019). Preregistering qualitative research, *Accountability in Research*, 26: 229–44. Available at https://doi.org/10.1080/08989621.2019.15801 47 (accessed 31 August 2022).

Hays, R.D., Weech-Maldonado, R., Teresi, J.A., Wallace, S.P. and Stewart, A.L. (2018). Commentary: Copyright restrictions versus open access to survey instruments, *Medical Care*, 56: 107–10. Available at https://doi.org/10.1097/MLR.0000000000000857 (accessed 31 August 2022).

Heene, M. and Ferguson, C.J. (2017). Psychological science's aversion to the null, and why many of the things you think are true, aren't, in S.O. Lilienfeld and I.D. Waldman (eds) *Psychological Science Under Scrutiny: Recent Challenges and Proposed Solutions*. John Wiley & Sons, pp. 34–52.

Heirene, R., LaPlante, D., Louderback, E.R. et al. (2021). Preregistration specificity and adherence: A review of preregistered gambling studies and cross-disciplinary comparison, *PsyArXiv*, 16 July. Available at https://doi.org/10.31234/osf.io/nj4es (accessed 31 August 2022).

Henderson, E.L., Simons, D.J. and Barr, D.J. (2021). The trajectory of truth: A longitudinal study of the illusory truth effect, *Journal of Cognition*, 4: 29. Available at https://dx.doi.org/10.5334%2Fjoc.161 (accessed 31 August 2022).

Higginson, A.D. and Munafò, M.R. (2016). Current incentives for scientists to lead underpowered studies with erroneous conclusions, *PLoS Biology*, 14: e2000995. Available at https://doi.org/10.1371/journal.pbio.2000995 (accessed 31 August 2022).

Hoekstra, R. and Vazire, S. (2021). Aspiring to greater intellectual humility in science, *Nature Human Behavior*, 5: 1602–7. Available at https://doi.org/10.1038/s41562-021-01203-8 (accessed 31 August 2022).

Hummer, L.T., Singleton Thorn, F., Nosek, B.A. and Errington, T.M. (2017). Evaluating Registered Reports: A naturalistic comparative study of article impact, *OSF Preprints*, 4 December. Available at https://doi.org/10.31219/osf.io/5y8w7 (accessed 31 August 2022).

Husnu, S. and Crisp, R.J. (2010). Elaboration enhances the imagined contact effect, *Journal of Experimental Social Psychology*, 46: 943–950. Available at https://doi.org/10.1016/j.jesp.2010.05.014 (accessed 31 August 2022).

Hussey, I. (2022). The best theory is a flawed one: Lessons from implicit bias research, *YouTube*, 14 February. Available at https://www.youtube.com/watch?v=GvZO_Xy5SdM&t=2165s (accessed 31 August 2022).

Hutson, M. (2018). Artificial intelligence faces reproducibility crisis, *Science*, 359: 725–6. Available at https://doi.org/10.1126/science.359.6377.725 (accessed 31 August 2022).

Inzlicht, M. (2016). Reckoning with the past. Getting better: random musings about science, psychology, and what-have-yous [blog], 29 February. Available at http://michaelinzlicht.com/getting-better/2016/2/29/reckoning-with-the-past (accessed 31 August 2022).

Ioannidis, J.P.A. (2005). Why most published research findings are false, *PLoS Medicine*, 2: e124. Available at https://doi.org/10.1371/journal.pmed.0020124 (accessed 31 August 2022).

Ioannidis, J.P.A. (2012). Why science isn't necessarily self-correcting, *Perspectives on Psychological Science*, 7, 645–54. Available at https://doi.org/10.1177%2F1745691612464056 (accessed 31 August 2022).

Ioannidis, J.P.A. (2018). Meta-research: Why research on research matters, *PLoS Biology*, 16: e2005468. Available at https://doi.org/10.1371/journal.pbio.2005468 (accessed 31 August 2022).

Ioannidis, J.P., Allison, D.B., Ball, C.A. et al. (2009). Repeatability of published microarray gene expression analyses, *Nature Genetics*, 41, 149–55. Available at https://doi.org/10.1038/ng.295 (accessed 31 August 2022).

Ioannidis, J.P.A., Fanelli, D., Dunne, D.D. and Goodman, S.N. (2015). Meta-research: Evaluation and improvement of research methods and practices, *PLoS Biology*, 13: e1002264. Available at https://doi.org/10.1371/journal.pbio.1002264 (accessed 31 August 2022).

Janke, S., Daumiller, M. and Rudert, S.C. (2018). Dark pathways to achievement in science: Researchers' achievement goals predict engagement in questionable research practices, *Social Psychological & Personality Science*, 10: 783–91. Available at https://doi.org/10.1177%2F1948550618790227 (accessed 31 August 2022).

Jarke, H., Jakob, L., Bojanić, L. et al. (2022). Registered Report: How open do you want your science? An international investigation into knowledge and attitudes of psychology students, *PLoS One*, 17: e0261260. Available at https://doi.org/10.1371/journal.pone.0261260 (accessed 31 August 2022).

Jekel, M., Fiedler, S., Allstadt Torras, R., Mischkowski, D., Dorrough, A.R. and Glöckner, A. (2020). How to teach open science principles in the undergraduate curriculum – The Hagen cumulative science project, *Psychology Learning & Teaching*, 19: 91–106. Available at https://doi.org/10.1177%2F1475725719868149 (accessed 31 August 2022).

John, L.K., Loewenstein, G. and Prelec, D. (2012). Measuring the prevalence of questionable research practices with incentives for truth telling, *Psychological Science*, 23: 524–32. Available at https://doi.org/10.1177%2F0956797611430953 (accessed 31 August 2022).

Jones, A., Worrall, S., Rudin, L., Duckworth, J.J. and Christiansen, P. (2021). May I have your attention, please? Methodological and analytical flexibility in the addiction Stroop, *Addiction Research & Theory*, 29: 413–26. Available at https://doi.org/10.1080/16066359.2021.1876847 (accessed 31 August 2022).

Jones, B.C., DeBruine, L.M., Flake, J.K. et al. (2021). To which world regions does the valence-dominance model of social perception apply?, *Nature Human Behavior*, 5, 159–69. Available at https://doi.org/10.1038/s41562-020-01007-2 (accessed 31 August 2022).

Junk, T.R. and Lyons, L. (2020). Reproducibility and replication of experimental particle physics results, *Harvard Data Science Review*, 2. Available at https://doi.org/10.1162/99608f92.250f995b (accessed 31 August 2022).

Kaplan, R.M. and Irvin, V.L. (2015). Likelihood of null effects of large NHLBI clinical trials has increased over time, *PLoS One*, 10: e0132382. Available at https://doi.org/10.1371/journal.pone.0132382 (accessed 31 August 2022).

Karhulahti, V. (2022). Reasons for qualitative psychologists to share human data, *British Journal of Social Psychology*. Available at https://doi.org/10.1111/bjso.12573.

Kathawalla, U.K., Silverstein, P. and Syed, M. (2021). Easing into open science: A guide for graduate students and their advisors, *Collabra: Psychology*, 7: 1–14. Available at https://doi.org/10.1525/collabra.18684 (accessed 31 August 2022).

Kerr, N.L. (1998). HARKing: Hypothesizing after the results are known, *Personality & Social Psychology Review*, 2: 196–217. Available at https://doi.org/10.1207%2Fs15327957pspr0203_4 (accessed 31 August 2022).

Kidwell, M.C., Lazarević, L.B., Baranski, E. et al. (2016). Badges to acknowledge open practices: A simple, low-cost, effective method for increasing transparency, *PLoS*

Biology, 14: e1002456. Available at https://doi.org/10.1371/journal.pbio.1002456 (accessed 31 August 2022).

Kiyonaga, A. and Scimeca, J.M. (2019). Practical considerations for navigating registered reports, *Trends in Neurosciences*, 42: 568–72. Available at https://doi.org/10.1016/j.tins.2019.07.003 (accessed 31 August 2022).

Klein, O., Hardwicke, T.E., Aust, F. et al. (2018a). A practical guide for transparency in psychological science, *Collabra: Psychology*, 4: 20. Available at https://doi.org/10.1525/collabra.158 (accessed 31 August 2022).

Klein, R.A., Cook, C.L., Ebersole, C.R. et al. (2022). Many Labs 4: Failure to replicate mortality salience effect with and without original author involvement, *Collabra: Psychology*, 8: 35271. Available at https://doi.org/10.1525/collabra.35271 (accessed 31 August 2022).

Klein, R.A., Ratliff, K.A., Vianelloa, M. et al. (2014). Investigating variation in replicability: A 'many labs' replication project, *Social Psychology*, 45: 142–52. Available at http://dx.doi.org/10.1027/1864-9335/a000178 (accessed 31 August 2022).

Klein, R.A., Vianello, M., Hasselman, F. et al. (2018b). Many Labs 2: Investigating variation in replicability across samples and settings, *Advances in Methods & Practices in Psychological Science*, 1: 443–90. Available at https://doi.org/10.1177/2515245918810225 (accessed 31 August 2022).

Koole, S.L. and Lakens, D. (2012). Rewarding replications: A sure and simple way to improve psychological science, *Perspectives on Psychological Science*, 7: 608–14. Available at https://doi.org/10.1177%2F1745691612462586 (accessed 31 August 2022).

Krishna, A. and Peter, S.M. (2018). Questionable research practices in student final theses – Prevalence, attitudes, and the role of the supervisor's perceived attitudes, *PLoS One*, 13: e0203470. Available at https://doi.org/10.1371/journal.pone.0203470 (accessed 31 August 2022).

Kuhn, T. (1962). *The Structure of Scientific Revolutions*. University of Chicago Press.

Lakatos, I. (1978). Falsification and the methodology of scientific research programmes, in J. Worrall and G. Currie (eds) *The Methodology of Scientific Research Programmes*. Cambridge University Press, pp. 8–101. Available at https://doi.org/10.1017/CBO9780511621123 (accessed 31 August 2022).

Lakens, D. (2013). Calculating and reporting effect sizes to facilitate cumulative science: A practical primer for *t*-tests and ANOVAs, *Frontiers in Psychology*, 863: 1–12. Available at https://doi.org/10.3389/fpsyg.2013.00863 (accessed 31 August 2022).

Lakens, D. (2014). Performing high-powered studies efficiently with sequential analyses, *European Journal of Social Psychology*, 44: 701–10. Available at https://doi.org/10.1002/ejsp.2023 (accessed 31 August 2022).

Lakens, D. (2019). The value of preregistration for psychological science: A conceptual analysis, *Japanese Psychological Review*, 62: 221–30.

Lakens, D. (2021). The practical alternative to the *p* value is the correctly used *p* value, *Perspectives on Psychological Science*, 16: 639–48. Available at https://doi.org/10.1177%2F1745691620958012 (accessed 31 August 2022).

Lakens, D. (2022). Sample size justification, *Collabra: Psychology*, 8: 33267. Available at https://doi.org/10.1525/collabra.33267 (accessed 31 August 2022).

Lakens, D., Adolfi, F.G., Albers, C.J. et al. (2018a). Justify your alpha, *Nature Human Behaviour*, 2: 168–71. Available at https://doi.org/10.1038/s41562-018-0311-x (accessed 31 August 2022).

Lakens, D., McLatchie, N., Isager, P.M., Scheel, A.M. and Dienes, Z. (2020). Improving inferences about null effects with Bayes factors and equivalence tests, *The Journals of Gerontology: Series B*, 75: 45–57. Available at https://doi.org/10.1093/geronb/gby065 (accessed 31 August 2022).

Lakens, D., Scheel, A.M. and Isager, P.M. (2018b). Equivalence testing for psychological research: A tutorial, *Advances in Methods & Practices in Psychological Science*, 2: 259–69. Available at https://doi.org/10.1177%2F2515245918770963 (accessed 31 August 2022).

Ledgerwood, A., Hudson, S.T.J., Lewis, N.A., Jr et al. (2022). The pandemic as a portal: Reimagining psychological science as truly open and inclusive, *Perspectives on Psychological Science* [advance online publication], 17: 937–59. Available at https://doi.org/10.1177%2F17456916211036654 (accessed 31 August 2022).

Leganes-Fonteneau, M., Bates, M.E., Muzumdar, N. et al. (2021). Cardiovascular mechanisms of interoceptive awareness: Effects of resonance breathing, *International Journal of Psychophysiology*, 169: 71–87. Available at https://doi.org/10.1016/j.ijpsycho.2021.09.003 (accessed 31 August 2022).

Levenstein, M.C. and Lyle, J.A. (2018). Data: Sharing is caring, *Advances in Methods & Practices in Psychological Science*, 1: 95–103. Available at https://doi.org/10.1177%2F2515245918758319 (accessed 31 August 2022).

Lieck, D.S.N. (2022). Examining psychologists' attitudes toward Big Team Science. Unpublished master's thesis, Albert-Ludwigs-Universität Freiburg, Freiburg, Germany.

Lieck, D.S.N. and Lakens, D. (2022). An overview of team science projects in the social behavioral sciences. *OSFHome*. Available at http://dx.doi.org/10.17605/OSF.IO/WX4ZD (accessed 31 August 2022).

Lilienfeld, S.O. and Strother, A.N. (2020). Psychological measurement and the replication crisis: Four sacred cows, *Canadian Psychology*, 61: 281–8. Available at https://doi.org/10.1037/cap0000236 (accessed 31 August 2022).

Lindley, D.V. (1957). A statistical paradox, *Biometrika*, 44: 187–92. Available at https://doi.org/10.1093/biomet/44.1-2.187 (accessed 31 August 2022).

Loken, E. and Gelman, A. (2017). Measurement error and the replication crisis, *Science*, 355: 584–5. Available at https://doi.org/10.1126/science.aal3618 (accessed 31 August 2022).

López-Nicolás, R., López-López, J.A., Rubio-Aparicio, M. and Sánchez-Meca, J. (2022). A meta-review of transparency and reproducibility-related reporting practices in published meta-analyses on clinical psychological interventions (2000–2020), *Behavior Research Methods*, 54: 334–49. Available at https://doi.org/10.3758/s13428-021-01644-z (accessed 31 August 2022).

Mahoney, M.J. (1977). Publication prejudices: An experimental study of confirmatory bias in the peer review system, *Cognitive Therapy & Research*, 1: 161–75. Available at https://doi.org/10.1007/BF01173636 (accessed 31 August 2022).

Maier, M. and Lakens, D. (2022). Justify your alpha: A primer on two practical approaches, *Advances in Methods and Practices in Psychological Science*, 5: 1–14. Available at https://doi.org/10.1177%2F25152459221080396 (accessed 31 August 2022).

Makel, M.C. and Plucker, J.A. (2014). Facts are more important than novelty: Replication in the education sciences, *Educational Researcher*, 43: 304–16. Available at https://doi.org/10.3102%2F0013189X14545513 (accessed 31 August 2022).

Makel, M.C., Plucker, J.A. and Hegarty, B. (2012). Replications in psychology research: How often do they really occur?, *Perspectives on Psychological Science*, 7: 537–42. Available at https://doi.org/10.1177/1745691612460688 (accessed 31 August 2022).

Marsh, A.A., Rhoads, S.A. and Ryan, R.M. (2019). A multi-semester classroom demonstration yields evidence in support of the facial feedback effect, *Emotion*, 19: 1500–4. Available at https://doi.org/10.1037/emo0000532 (accessed 31 August 2022).

Mathieu, S., Chan, A.W. and Ravaud, P. (2013). Use of trial register information during the peer review process, *PLoS One*, 8: 2–5. Available at https://doi.org/10.1371/journal.pone.0059910 (accessed 31 August 2022).

Maxwell, S.E. (2004). The persistence of underpowered studies in psychological research: Causes, consequences, and remedies, *Psychological Methods*, 9: 147–63. Available at https://doi.org/10.1037/1082-989x.9.2.147 (accessed 31 August 2022).

Maxwell, S.E., Lau, M.Y. and Howard, G.S. (2015). Is psychology suffering from a replication crisis? What does 'failure to replicate' really mean?, *American Psychologist*, 70: 487–98. Available at https://doi.org/10.1037/a0039400 (accessed 31 August 2022).

McCarthy, R.J., Skowronski, J.J., Verschuere, B. et al. (2018). Registered replication report on Srull and Wyer (1979), *Advances in Methods & Practices in Psychological Science*, 1: 321–36. Available at https://doi.org/10.1177/2515245918777487 (accessed 31 August 2022).

McKiernan, E.C., Bourne, P.E., Titus Brown, C. et al. (2016). How open science helps researchers succeed, *eLife*, 5: e16800. Available at https://doi.org/10.7554/eLife.16800 (accessed 31 August 2022).

Meehl, P.E. (1967). Theory-testing in psychology and physics: A methodological paradox, *Philosophy of Science*, 34: 103–15. Available at https://doi.org/10.1086/288135 (accessed 31 August 2022).

Merten, G. and Krypotos, A.-M. (2019). Preregistration of analyses of preexisting data, *Journal of the Belgian Association for Psychological Science*, 59: 338–52. Available at http://doi.org/10.5334/pb.493 (accessed 31 August 2022).

Merton, R.K. (1973). *The Sociology of Science: Theoretical and Empirical Investigations*. University of Chicago Press.

Meyer, M.N. (2018). Practical tips for ethical data sharing, *Advances in Methods & Practices in Psychological Science*, 1: 131–44. Available at https://doi.org/10.1177%2F2515245917747656 (accessed 31 August 2022).

Miyakwa, T. (2020). No raw data, no science: Another possible source of the reproducibility crisis, *Molecular Brain*, 13: 1–6. Available at https://doi.org/10.1186/s13041-020-0552-2 (accessed 31 August 2022).

Mol, J.M., Botzen, W.J.W. and Blasch, J.E. (2022). After the virtual flood: Risk perceptions and flood preparedness after virtual reality risk communication, *Judgement & Decision Making*, 17: 189–214.

Moon, A. and Roeder, S.S. (2014). A secondary replication attempt of stereotype susceptibility (Shih, Pittinsky, and Ambady, 1999), *Social Psychology*, 45: 199–201. Available at https://doi.org/10.1027/1864-9335/a000193 (accessed 31 August 2022).

Moshontz, H., Binion, G., Walton, H., Brown, B.T. and Syed, M. (2021). A guide to posting and managing preprints, *Advances in Methods & Practices in Psychological Science*, 4: 1–11. Available at https://doi.org/10.1177%2F25152459211019948 (accessed 31 August 2022).

Moshontz, H., Campbell, L., Ebersole, C.R. et al. (2018). The Psychological Science Accelerator: Advancing psychology through a distributed collaborative network, *Advances in Methods & Practices in Psychological Science*, 1: 501–15. Available at https://doi.org/10.1177%2F2515245918797607 (accessed 31 August 2022).

Mueller-Langer, F., Fecher, B., Harhoff, D. and Wagner, G.G. (2019). Replication studies in economics: How many and which papers are chosen for replication, and why?, *Research Policy*, 48: 62–83. Available at https://doi.org/10.1016/j.respol.2018.07.019 (accessed 31 August 2022).

Munafò, M.R., Chambers, C.D., Collins, A.M., Fortunato, L. and Macleod, M.R. (2020). Research culture and reproducibility, *Trends in Cognitive Sciences*, 24: 91–3. Available at https://doi.org/10.1016/j.tics.2019.12.002 (accessed 31 August 2022).

Munafò, M.R., Chambers, C., Collins, A., Fortunato, L. and Macleod, M. (2022). The reproducibility debate is an opportunity, not a crisis, *BMC Research Notes*, 15: 1–3. Available at https://doi.org/10.1186/s13104-022-05942-3 (accessed 31 August 2022).

Munafò, M.R., Nosek, B.A., Bishop, D.V.M. et al. (2017). A manifesto for reproducible science, *Nature Human Behaviour*, 1: 1–9. Available at https://doi.org/10.1038/s41562-016-0021 (accessed 31 August 2022).

Murphy, M.C., Mejia, A.F., Mejia, J. et al. (2020). Open science, communal culture, and women's participation in the movement to improve science, *Proceedings of the National Academic of Sciences*, 117: 24154–64. Available at https://doi.org/10.1073/pnas.1921320117 (accessed 31 August 2022).

National Academies of Sciences, Engineering, and Medicine (2019). *Reproducibility and Replicability in Science*. National Academies Press. Available at https://doi.org/10.17226/25303 (accessed 31 August 2022).

Noah, T., Schul, Y. and Mayo, R. (2018). When both the original study and its failed replication are correct: Feeling observed eliminates the facial-feedback effect, *Journal of Personality & Social Psychology*, 114: 657–64. Available at http://dx.doi.org/10.1037/pspa0000121 (accessed 31 August 2022).

Norris, E. and O'Connor, D.B. (2019). Science as a behaviour: Using a behaviour change approach to increase uptake of open science, *Psychology & Health*, 34: 1397–406. Available at https://doi.org/10.1080/08870446.2019.1679373 (accessed 31 August 2022).

Nosek, B.A. (2017). Why are we working so hard to open up science? A personal story, *Center for Open Science* [blog], 8 December. Available at https://www.cos.io/blog/why-are-we-working-so-hard-open-science-personal-story (accessed 31 August 2022).

Nosek, B.A., Alter, G., Banks, G.C. et al. (2015). Promoting an open research culture: Author guidelines for journals could help to promote transparency, openness, and reproducibility, *Science*, 348: 1422–5. Available at https://dx.doi.org/10.1126%2F-science.aab2374 (accessed 31 August 2022).

Nosek, B.A., Banaji, M.R. and Greenwald, A.G. (2002). Math = male, me = female, therefore math ≠ me, *Journal of Personality & Social Psychology*, 83: 44–59. Available at https://doi.org/10.1037//0022-3514.83.1.44 (accessed 31 August 2022).

Nosek, B.A. and Bar-Anan, Y. (2012). Scientific utopia: I. Opening scientific communication, *Psychological Inquiry*, 23: 217–43. Available at https://doi.org/10.1080/1047840X.2012.692215 (accessed 31 August 2022).

Nosek, B.A., Beck, E.D., Campbell, L. et al. (2019). Preregistration is hard, and worthwhile, *Trends in Cognitive Sciences*, 23: 815–18. Available at https://doi.org/10.1016/j.tics.2019.07.009 (accessed 31 August 2022).

Nosek, B.A., Ebersole, C.R., DeHaven, A.C. and Mellor, D.T. (2018). The preregistration revolution, *Proceedings of the National Academy of Sciences*, 115: 2600–6. Available at https://doi.org/10.1073/pnas.1708274114 (accessed 31 August 2022).

Nosek, B.A. and Errington, T.M. (2017). Reproducibility in cancer biology: Making sense of replications, *eLife*, 6: e23383. Available at https://doi.org/10.7554/eLife.23383 (accessed 31 August 2022).

Nosek, B.A., Hardwicke, T.E., Moshontz, H. et al. (2021). Replicability, robustness, and reproducibility in psychological science, *Annual Review of Psychology*, 73: 719–48. Available at https://doi.org/10.1146/annurev-psych-020821-114157 (accessed 31 August 2022).

Nosek, B.A. and Lakens, D. (2014). Registered reports: A method to increase the credibility of published results, *Social Psychology*, 45: 137–41. Available at https://doi.org/10.1027/1864-9335/a000192 (accessed 31 August 2022).

Nosek, B.A. and Lindsay, D.S. (2018). Preregistration becoming the norm in psychological science, *APS Observer*, 28 February. Available at https://www.psychologicalscience.org/observer/preregistration-becoming-the-norm-in-psychological-science (accessed 31 August 2022).

O'Boyle, E.H. Jr, Banks, G.C. and Gonzalez-Mulé, E. (2017). The chrysalis effect: How ugly initial results metamorphosize into beautiful articles, *Journal of Management*, 43: 376–99. Available at https://doi.org/10.1177/0149206314527133 (accessed 31 August 2022).

Obels, P., Lakens, D., Coles, N.A., Gottfried, J. and Green, S.A. (2020). Analysis of open data and computational reproducibility in Registered Reports in psychology, *Advances in Methods & Practices in Psychological Science*, 3: 229–37. Available at https://doi.org/10.1177%2F2515245920918872 (accessed 31 August 2022).

O'Connor, D.B. (2021). Leonardo da Vinci, preregistration and the architecture of science: Towards a more open and transparent research culture, *Health Psychology Bulletin*, 5: 39–45. Available at http://doi.org/10.5334/hpb.30 (accessed 31 August 2022).

Open Science Collaboration (2012). An open, large-scale, collaborative effort to estimate the reproducibility of psychological science, *Perspectives on Psychological Science*, 7, 657–60. Available at https://doi.org/10.1177%2F1745691612462588 (accessed 31 August 2022).

Open Science Collaboration (2015). Estimating the reproducibility of psychological science, *Science*, 349: aac4716. Available at https://doi.org/10.1126/science.aac4716 (accessed 31 August 2022).

Oppenheimer, D.M. and Monin, B. (2009). The retrospective gambler's fallacy: Unlikely events, constructing the past, and multiple universes, *Judgment & Decision Making*, 4: 326–34.

Page, M.J., Shamseer, L. and Tricco, A.C. (2018). Registration of systematic reviews in PROSPERO: 30,000 records and counting, *Systematic Reviews*, 7: 1–9. Available at https://doi.org/10.1186/s13643-018-0699-4 (accessed 31 August 2022).

Parsons, S., Azevedo, F., Elsherif, M.M.M. et al. (2022). A community-sourced glossary of open scholarship terms, *Nature Human Behaviour*, 6: 312–18. Available at https://doi.org/10.1038/s41562-021-01269-4 (accessed 31 August 2022).

Pashler, H. and Wagenmakers, E.-J. (2012). Editors' introduction to the special section on replicability in psychological science: A crisis of confidence?, *Perspectives on Psychological Science*, 7: 528–30. Available at https://doi.org/10.1177%2F1745691612465253 (accessed 31 August 2022).

Pavlov, Y.G., Adamian, N., Appelhoff, S. et al. (2021). #EEGManyLabs: Investigating the replicability of influential EEG experiments, *Cortex*, 144: 213–29. Available at https://doi.org/10.1016/j.cortex.2021.03.013 (accessed 31 August 2022).

Peirce, J.W., Gray, J.R., Simpson, S. et al. (2019). PsychoPy2: Experiments in behavior made easy, *Behavior Research Methods*, 51: 195–203. Available at https://doi.org/10.3758/s13428-018-01193-y (accessed 31 August 2022).

Peng, R. (2015). The reproducibility crisis in science: A statistical counterattack, *Significance*, 12: 30–2. Available at https://doi.org/10.1111/j.1740-9713.2015.00827.x (accessed 31 August 2022).

Pennington, C.R. and Heim, D. (2022). Reshaping the publication process: Addiction Research and Theory joins Peer Community In Registered Reports, *Addiction, Research & Theory*, 30: 1–4. Available at https://doi.org/10.1080/16066359.2021.1931142 (accessed 31 August 2022).

Pennington, C.R., Heim, D., Levy, A.R. and Larkin, D.T. (2016). Twenty years of stereotype threat research: A review of psychological mediators, *PLoS One*, 11: e0146487. Available at https://doi.org/10.1371/journal.pone.0146487 (accessed 31 August 2022).

Pennington, C.R., Jones, A., Bartlett, J.E., Copeland, A. and Shaw, D.J. (2021). Raising the bar: Improving methodological rigour in cognitive alcohol research, *Addiction*, 116: 3243–51. Available at https://doi.org/10.1111/add.15563 (accessed 31 August 2022).

Pennington, C.R., Jones, A.J., Tzavella, L., Chambers, C.D. and Button, K.S. (2022). Beyond online crowdsourcing: The benefits and opportunities of big team science, *Experimental & Clinical Psychopharmacology*, 30: 444–51. Available at https://doi.org/10.1037/pha0000541 (accessed 31 August 2022).

Pham, M.T. and Oh, T.T. (2021a). Preregistration is neither sufficient nor necessary for good science, *Journal of Consumer Psychology*, 31: 163–76. Available at https://doi.org/10.1002/jcpy.1209 (accessed 31 August 2022).

Pham, M.T. and Oh, T.T. (2021b). On not confusing the tree of trustworthy statistics with the greater forest of good science: A comment on Simmons et al.'s perspective on pre-registration, *Journal of Consumer Psychology*, 31: 181–5. Available at https://doi.org/10.1002/jcpy.1213 (accessed 31 August 2022).

Piwowar, H.A. and Vision, T.J. (2013). Data reuse and the open data citation advantage, *PeerJ*, 1: e175. Available at https://doi.org/10.7717/peerj.175 (accessed 31 August 2022).

Poldrack, R. (2013). Anatomy of a coding error, russpoldrack.org, 20 February. Available at http://www.russpoldrack.org/2013/02/anatomy-of-coding-error.html (accessed 31 August 2022).

Popper, K.R. (2002 [1959]). *The Logic of Scientific Discovery*, Classic Series. Routledge.

Pownall, M. (2020). Pre-registration in the undergraduate dissertation: A critical discussion, *Psychology Teaching Review*, 26, 71–6.

Pownall, M., Azevedo, F., König, L.M. et al. (2022). The impact of open and reproducible scholarship on students' scientific literacy, engagement, and attitudes towards science: A review and synthesis of the evidence, *MetaArXiv*, 8 April. Available at https://doi.org/10.31222/osf.io/9e526 (accessed 31 August 2022).

Pownall, M., Talbot, C.V., Henschel, A. et al. (2021). Navigating open science as early career feminist researchers, *Psychology of Women Quarterly*, 45: 526–39. Available at https://doi.org/10.1177%2F03616843211029255 (accessed 31 August 2022).

Prosser, A.M.B., Hamshaw, R., Meyer, J. et al. (2022). When open data closes the door: A critical examination of the past, present and the potential future for open data guidelines in journals. *British Journal of Social Psychology*. Available at https://doi.org/10.1111/bjso.12576.

Protzko, J., Krosnick, J., Nelson, L.D. et al. (2020). High replicability of newly-discovered social-behavioral findings is achievable, *PsyArXiv*, 10 September. Available at https://doi.org/10.31234/osf.io/n2a9x (accessed 31 August 2022).

Pusztai, L., Hatzis, C. and Andre, F. (2013). Reproducibility of research and preclinical validation: Problems and solutions, *Nature Reviews Clinical Oncology*, 10: 720–4. Available at http://www.nature.com/doifinder/10.1038/nrclinonc.2013.171 (accessed 31 August 2022).

Quintana, D.S. (2020). A synthetic dataset primer for the biobehavioural sciences to promote reproducibility and hypothesis generation, *eLife*, 9: e53275. Available at https://doi.org/10.7554/eLife.53275 (accessed 31 August 2022).

Redish, A.D., Kummerfeld, E., Morris, R.L. and Love, A.C. (2018). Opinion: Reproducibility failures are essential to scientific inquiry, *Proceedings of the National Academy of Sciences of the United States of America*, 115: 5042–6. Available at https://doi.org/10.1073/pnas.1806370115 (accessed 31 August 2022).

Richards, K.A. and Hemphill, M.A. (2017). A practical guide to collaborative qualitative data analysis, *Journal of Teaching in Physical Education*, 37: 225–31. Available at https://doi.org/10.1123/jtpe.2017-0084 (accessed 31 August 2022).

Ritchie, S. (2020). *Science Fictions: Exposing Fraud, Bias, Negligence and Hype in Science*. Random House.

Ritchie, S.J., Wiseman, R. and French, C.C. (2012). Failing the future: Three unsuccessful attempts to replicate Bem's 'Retroactive Facilitation of Recall' effect, *PLoS One*, 7: e33423. Available at https://doi.org/10.1371/journal.pone.0033423 (accessed 31 August 2022).

Robson, S.G., Baum, M.A., Beaudry, J.L. et al. (2021). Promoting open science: A holistic approach to changing behaviour, *Collabra: Psychology*, 7: 30137. Available at https://doi.org/10.1525/collabra.30137 (accessed 31 August 2022).

Rohrer, J. (2021). A self-correcting fallacy: Why don't researchers correct their own errors in the scientific record?, *LSE Impact Blog*, 13 April. Available at https://blogs.lse.ac.uk/impactofsocialsciences/2021/04/13/a-self-correcting-fallacy-why-dont-researchers-correct-their-own-errors-in-the-scientific-record/ (accessed 31 August 2022).

Rohrer, J.M., Tierney, W., Uhlmann, E.L. et al. (2021). Putting the self in self-correction: Findings from the loss-of-confidence project, *Perspectives on Psychological Science*, 16: 1255–69. Available at https://doi.org/10.1177%2F1745691620964106 (accessed 31 August 2022).

Romero, F. (2017). Novelty versus replicability: Virtues and vices in the reward system of science, *Philosophy of Science*, 84: 1031–43. Available at https://doi.org/10.1086/694005 (accessed 31 August 2022).

Rosenthal, R. (1966). *Experimenter Effects in Behavioral Research*. Appleton-Century-Crofts.

Rosenthal, R. (1979). The file drawer problem and tolerance for null results, *Psychological Bulletin*, 86: 638–41. Available at https://doi.org/10.1037//0033-2909.86.3.638 (accessed 31 August 2022).

Ross, M.W., Iguchi, M.Y. and Panicker, S. (2018). Ethical aspects of data sharing and research participant protections, *American Psychologist*, 73: 138–45. Available at http://dx.doi.org/10.1037/amp0000240 (accessed 31 August 2022).

Rouder, J.N. (2016). The what, why, and how of born-open data, *Behavior Research Methods*, 48: 1062–9. Available at https://doi.org/10.3758/s13428-015-0630-z (accessed 31 August 2022).

Rubin, M. (2017). When does HARKing hurt? Identifying when different types of undisclosed post hoc hypothesizing harm scientific progress, *Review of General Psychology*, 21: 308–20. Available at https://doi.org/10.1037/gpr0000128 (accessed 31 August 2022).

Scheel, A.M., Schijen, M.R.M.J. and Lakens, D. (2021). An excess of positive results: Comparing the standard psychology literature with Registered Reports, *Advances in Methods & Practices in Psychological Science*, 4: 1–12. Available at https://doi.org/10.1177%2F25152459211007467 (accessed 31 August 2022).

Schmidt, S. (2009). Shall we really do it again? The powerful concept of replication is neglected in the social sciences, *Review of General Psychology*, 13: 90–100. Available at https://doi.org/10.1037%2Fa0015108 (accessed 31 August 2022).

Shewach, O.R., Sackett, P.R. and Quint, S. (2019). Stereotype threat effects in settings with features likely versus unlikely in operational test settings: A meta-analysis, *Journal of Applied Psychology*, 104: 1514–34. Available at https://doi.org/10.1037/apl0000420 (accessed 31 August 2022).

Sijtsma, K. (2016). Playing with data – or how to discourage questionable research practices and stimulate researchers to do things right, *Psychometrika*, 81: 1–15. Available at https://doi.org/10.1007/s11336-015-9446-0 (accessed 31 August 2022).

Silberzahn, R., Uhlmann, E.L., Martin, D.P. et al. (2018). Many analysts, one data set: Making transparent how variations in analytical choices affect results, *Advances in Methods & Practices in Psychological Science*, 1: 337–56. Available at https://doi.org/10.1177%2F2515245917747646 (accessed 31 August 2022).

Simmons, J.P., Nelson, L.D. and Simonsohn, U. (2011). False-positive psychology: Undisclosed flexibility in data collection and analysis allows presenting anything as significant, *Psychological Science*, 22, 1359–66. Available at https://doi.org/ 10.1177%2F0956797611417632 (accessed 31 August 2022).

Simmons, J.P., Nelson, L.D. and Simonsohn, U. (2018). False-positive citations, *Perspectives on Psychological Science*, 13: 255–9. Available at https://doi. org/10.1177%2F1745691617698146 (accessed 31 August 2022).

Simmons, J.P., Nelson, L.D. and Simonsohn, U. (2020a). Pre-registration: Why and how, *Journal of Consumer Psychology*, 31: 151–62. Available at https://doi.org/10.1002/ jcpy.1208 (accessed 31 August 2022).

Simmons, J.P., Nelson, L.D. and Simonsohn, U. (2020b). Pre-registration is a game changer. But, like random assignment, it is neither necessary nor sufficient for credible science, *Journal of Consumer Psychology*, 31: 177–80. Available at https://doi. org/10.1002/jcpy.1207 (accessed 31 August 2022).

Simons, D.J. (2014). The value of direct replication, *Perspectives on Psychological Science*, 9: 76–80. Available at https://doi.org/10.1177%2F1745691613514755 (accessed 31 August 2022).

Simons, D.K., Holcombe, A.O. and Spellman, B.A. (2014). An introduction to Registered Replication Reports at *Perspectives on Psychological Science, Perspectives on Psychological Science*, 9: 552–5. Available at https://doi.org/10.1177%2F1745691614543974 (accessed 31 August 2022).

Skorich, D.P., Webb, H., Stewart, L. et al. (2013). Stereotype threat and hazard perception among provisional license drivers, *Accident Analysis & Prevention*, 54: 39–45. Available at https://doi.org/10.1016/j.aap.2013.02.002 (accessed 31 August 2022).

Smaldino, P.E. and McElreath, R. (2016). The natural selection of bad science, *Royal Society Open Science*, 3: 160384. Available at http://dx.doi.org/10.1098/rsos.160384 (accessed 31 August 2022).

Soderberg, C.K. (2018). Using OSF to share data: A step-by-step guide, *Advances in Methods & Practices in Psychological Science*, 1: 115–20. Available at https://doi. org/10.1177/2515245918757689 (accessed 31 August 2022).

Soderberg, C.K., Errington, T.M., Schiavone, S.R. et al. (2021). Initial evidence of research quality of Registered Reports compared with the standard publishing model, *Nature Human Behaviour*, 5: 990–7. Available at https://doi.org/10.1038/s41562-021-01142-4 (accessed 31 August 2022).

Spellman, B.A. (2015). A short (personal) future history of revolution 2.0, *Perspectives on Psychological Science*, 10: 886–99. Available at https://doi.org/ 10.1177%2F1745691615609918 (accessed 31 August 2022).

Spencer, S.J., Steele, C.M. and Quinn, D.M. (1999). Stereotype threat and women's math performance, *Journal of Experimental Social Psychology*, 35: 4–28. Available at https://doi.org/10.1006/jesp.1998.1373 (accessed 31 August 2022).

Spitschan, M., Rumsey, S., Jaquiery, M. and Galizzi, M.M. (2020). Preprints: A primer from UKRN, *OSF Preprints*, 30 October. Available at https://doi.org/10.31219/osf.io/m4zyh (accessed 31 August 2022).

Srull, T.K. and Wyer, R.S. (1979). The role of category accessibility in the interpretation of information about persons: Some determinants and implications, *Journal of Personality & Social Psychology*, 37: 1660–72. Available at https://doi.org/10.1037/0022-3514.37.10.1660 (accessed 31 August 2022).

Stapel, D. (2014). *Faking Science: A True Story of Academic Fraud* (trans. N. Brown). Available at http://nick.brown.free.fr/stapel (accessed 31 August 2022).

Steele, C.M. and Aronson, J. (1995). Stereotype threat and the intellectual test performance of African Americans, *Journal of Personality & Social Psychology*, 69:

797–811. Available at https://doi.org/10.1037//0022-3514.69.5.797 (accessed 31 August 2022).

Steltenpohl, C.N., Montilla Doble, L.J., Basnight-Brown, D.M. et al. (2021). Society for the improvement of psychological science global engagement task force report, *Collabra: Psychology*, 7: 22968. Available at https://doi.org/10.1525/collabra.22968 (accessed 31 August 2022).

Sterling, T.D. (1959). Publication decisions and their possible effects on inferences drawn from tests of significance – or vice versa, *Journal of the American Statistical Association*, 54: 30–4. Available at https://doi.org/10.1080/01621459.1959.10501497 (accessed 31 August 2022).

Stewart, L., Moher, D. and Shekelle, P. (2012). Why prospective registration of systematic reviews makes sense, *Systematic Reviews*, 1: 1–4. Available at https://doi.org/10.1186/2046-4053-1-7 (accessed 31 August 2022).

Stewart, S., Pennington, C.R., Silva, G. et al. (2022). Reforms to improve reproducibility and quality must be coordinated across the research ecosystem: The view from the UKRN Local Network Leads, *BMC Research Notes*, 15: 1–5. Available at https://doi.org/10.1186/s13104-022-05949-w (accessed 31 August 2022).

Stewart, S., Rinke, E., McGarrigle, R. et al. (2020). Pre-registration and Registered Reports: A primer from UKRN, *OSF Preprints*, 30 October. Available at https://doi.org/10.31219/osf.io/8v2n7 (accessed 31 August 2022).

Stodden, V., Seiler, J. and Ma, Z. (2018). An empirical analysis of journal policy effectiveness for computational reproducibility, *Proceedings of the National Academy of Sciences*, 115: 2584–9. Available at https://doi.org/10.1073/pnas.1708290115 (accessed 31 August 2022).

Strack, F. (2016). Reflection on the smiling Registered Replication Report, *Perspectives on Psychological Science*, 11: 929–30. Available at https://doi.org/10.1177%2F1745691616674460 (accessed 31 August 2022).

Strack, F., Martin, L.L. and Stepper, S. (1988). Inhibiting and facilitating conditions of the human smile: A nonobtrusive test of the facial feedback hypothesis, *Journal of Personality & Social Psychology*, 54: 768–77. Available at https://doi.org/10.1037/0022-3514.54.5.768 (accessed 31 August 2022).

Strand, J.F. and Brown, V.A. (2019). Publishing open, reproducible research with undergraduates, *Frontiers in Psychology*, 20: 564. Available at https://dx.doi.org/10.3389%2Ffpsyg.2019.00564 (accessed 31 August 2022).

Stroebe, W. and Strack, F. (2014). The alleged crisis and the illusion of exact replication, *Perspectives on Psychological Science*, 9: 59–71. Available at https://doi.org/10.1177%2F1745691613514450 (accessed 31 August 2022).

Sweeney, L. (2000). *Simple Demographics often Identify People Uniquely*. Carnegie Mellon University, Data Privacy Working Paper 3. Data Privacy Lab. Available at https://dataprivacylab.org/projects/identifiability/ (accessed 31 August 2022).

Szucs, D. and Ioannidis, J.P. (2017). Empirical assessment of published effect sizes and power in the recent cognitive neuroscience and psychology literature, *PLoS Biology*, 15: e2000797. Available at https://doi.org/10.1371/journal.pbio.2000797 (accessed 31 August 2022).

TARG Meta-Research Group and Collaborators (2021). Estimating the prevalence of discrepancies between study registrations and publications: A systematic review and meta-analyses, *MedRxiv*, 9 August. Available at https://doi.org/10.1101/2021.07.07.21259868 (accessed 31 August 2022).

TARG Meta-Research Group and Collaborators (2022). Discrepancy review: A feasibility study of a novel peer review intervention to reduce undisclosed discrepancies between registrations and publications. *Royal Society Open Science*, 9, 220142. Available at https://doi.org/10.1098/rsos.220142 (accessed 31 August 2022).

Tennant, J.P., Waldner, F., Jacques, D.C., Masuzzo, P., Collister, L.B. and Hartgerink, C.H. (2016). The academic, economic and societal impacts of Open Access: An evidence-based review, *F1000 Research*, 5: 632. Available at https://doi.org/10.12688/f1000research.8460.3 (accessed 31 August 2022).

Thornton, A. and Lee, P. (2000). Publication bias in meta-analysis: Its causes and consequences, *Journal of Clinical Epidemiology*, 53: 207–16. Available at https://doi.org/10.1016/s0895-4356(99)00161-4 (accessed 31 August 2022).

Tijdink, J.K., Bouter, L.M., Veldkamp, C.L.S., van de Ven, P.M., Wicherts, J.M. and Smulders, Y.M. (2016). Personality traits are associated with research misbehavior in Dutch scientists: A cross-sectional study, *PLoS One*, 11: e0163251. Available at https://doi.org/10.1371/journal.pone.0163251 (accessed 31 August 2022).

Trafimow, D. and Marks, M. (2014). Editorial, *Basic & Applied Social Psychology*, 37: 1–2. Available at https://doi.org/10.1080/01973533.2015.1012991 (accessed 31 August 2022).

Tukey, J.W. (1969). Analyzing data: Sanctification or detective work?, *American Psychologist*, 24: 83–91. Available at https://doi.org/10.1037/h0027108 (accessed 31 August 2022).

Turner, A., Topor, M., Stewart, A.J. et al. (2020). Open Code and Software: A primer from UKRN, *OSF Preprints*, 30 October. Available at https://doi.org/10.31219/osf.io/qw9ck (accessed 31 August 2022).

Tversky, A. and Kahneman, D. (1981). The framing of decisions and the psychology of choice, *Science*, 211: 453–8. Available at https://doi.org/10.1126/science.7455683 (accessed 31 August 2022).

Tzavella, L., Lawrence, N.S., Button, K.S. et al. (2021). Effects of go/no-go training on food-related action tendencies, liking and choice, *Royal Society Open Science*, 8: 210666. Available at https://doi.org/10.1098/rsos.210666 (accessed 31 August 2022).

UKRN Steering Committee (2021). From grassroots to global: A blueprint for building a reproducibility network, *PLoS Biology*, 9: e3001461. Available at https://doi.org/10.1371/journal.pbio.3001461 (accessed 31 August 2022).

van den Akker, O., Weston, S.J., Campbell, L. et al. (2021a). Preregistration of secondary data analysis: A template and tutorial, *Meta Psychology*, 5: 1–19. Available at https://doi.org/10.15626/MP.2020.2625 (accessed 31 August 2022).

van den Akker, O. et al. (2021b). The effectiveness of preregistration in psychology [conference presentation]. Metascience 2021 conference, 25 September. Available at https://osf.io/6qsf4/ (accessed 31 August 2022).

van der Zee, T., Anaya, J. and Brown, N.J.L. (2017). Statistical heartburn: An attempt to digest four pizza publications from the Cornell Food and Brand Lab, *BMC Nutrition*, 3: 54. Available at https://doi.org/10.1186/s40795-017-0167-x (accessed 31 August 2022).

van 't Veer, A.E. and Giner-Sorolla, R. (2016). Pre-registration in social psychology – A discussion and suggested template, *Journal of Experimental Social Psychology*, 67: 2–12. Available at https://doi.org/10.1016/j.jesp.2016.03.004 (accessed 31 August 2022).

van 't Veer, A., Simons, D.J., Mellor, D.T., Vazire, S., Corker, K.S. and Lindsay, D.S. (2019). APS 2019 preregistration workshop, *OSFHome*. Available at https://osf.io/4acje/ (accessed 31 August 2022).

Vanpaemel, W., Vermorgen, M., Deriemaecker, L. and Storms, G. (2015). Are we wasting a good crisis? The availability of psychological research data after the storm, *Collabra: Psychology*, 1: 1–5. Available at https://doi.org/10.1525/collabra.13 (accessed 31 August 2022).

Vazire, S. (2018). Implications of the credibility revolution for productivity, creativity, and progress, *Perspectives on Psychological Science*, 13: 411–17. Available at https://doi.org/10.1177%2F1745691617751884 (accessed 31 August 2022).

Vazire, S. (2019). Do we want to be credible or incredible?, *APS Observer*, 23 December. Available at https://www.psychologicalscience.org/observer/do-we-want-to-be-credible-or-incredible (accessed 31 August 2022).

Vazire, S. (2020). A toast to the error detectors, *Nature*, 577: 9. Available at https://doi.org/10.1038/d41586-019-03909-2 (accessed 31 August 2022).

Vazire, S. and Holcombe, A.O. (2021). Where are the self-correcting mechanisms in science?, *Review of General Psychology*, 16: 1255–69. Available at https://doi.org/10.1177/10892680211033912 (accessed 31 August 2022).

Verschuere, B., Meijer, E.H., Jim, A. et al. (2018). Registered Replication Report on Mazar, Amir, and Ariely (2008), *Advances in Methods & Practices in Psychological Science*, 1: 299–317. Available at https://doi.org/10.1177/2515245918781032 (accessed 31 August 2022).

Vohs, K.D., Schmeichel, B.J., Lohman, S. et al. (2021). A multisite preregistered paradigmatic test of the ego-depletion effect, *Psychological Science*, 32: 1566–81. Available at https://doi.org/10.1177%2F0956797621989733 (accessed 31 August 2022).

Wagenmakers, E.-J., Beek, T., Dijkhoff, L. et al. (2016). Registered Replication Report: Strack, Martin, and Stepper (1988), *Perspectives on Psychological Science*, 11: 917–28. Available at https://doi.org/10.1177%2F1745691616674458 (accessed 31 August 2022).

Wagenmakers, E.-J., Wetzels, R., Boorsboom, D. and van der Maas, H. (2011). Why psychologists must change the way they analyze their data: The case of Psi: Comment on Bem (2011), *Journal of Personality & Social Psychology*, 100: 426–32. Available at https://psycnet.apa.org/doi/10.1037/a0022790 (accessed 31 August 2022).

Wagenmakers, E.-J., Wetzels, R., Boorsboom, D., van der Maas, H.L.J. and Kievit, R.D. (2012). An agenda for purely confirmatory research, *Perspectives on Psychological Science*, 7: 632–8. Available at https://doi.org/10.1177%2F1745691612463078 (accessed 31 August 2022).

Wagge, J.R., Baciu, C., Banas, K. et al. (2019a). A demonstration of the collaborative replication and education project: Replication attempts of the red-romance effect, *Collabra: Psychology*, 5: 5. Available at https://doi.org/10.1525/collabra.177 (accessed 31 August 2022).

Wagge, J.R., Brandt, M.J., Lazarevic, L.B. et al. (2019b). Publishing research with undergraduate students via replication work: The Collaborative Replications and Education Project, *Frontiers in Psychology*, 10: 247. Available at https://doi.org/10.3389/fpsyg.2019.00247 (accessed 31 August 2022).

Walsh, C.G., Xia, W., Li, M., Denny, J.C., Harris, P.A. and Malin, B.A. (2018). Enabling open-science initiatives in clinical psychology and psychiatry without sacrificing patients' privacy: Current practices and future challenges, *Advances in Methods & Practices in Psychological Science*, 1: 104–14. Available at https://doi.org/10.1177/2515245917749652 (accessed 31 August 2022).

Walster, W.G. and Cleary, A.T. (1970). A proposal for a new editorial policy in the social sciences, *American Statistician*, 24: 16–19. Available at https://doi.org/10.1080/00031305.1970.10478884 (accessed 31 August 2022).

Wang, K., Goldenberg, A., Dorison, C.A. et al. (2021). A multi-country test of brief reappraisal interventions on emotions during the COVID-19 pandemic, *Nature*, 5: 1089–110. Available at https://doi.org/10.1038/s41562-021-01173-x (accessed 31 August 2022).

Wasserstein, R.L., Schirm, A.L. and Lazar, N.A. (2019). Moving to a world beyond '$p < 0.05$', *The American Statistician*, 73: 1–19. Available at https://doi.org/10.1080/00031305.2019.1583913 (accessed 31 August 2022).

Whitaker, K. and Guest, O. (2020). #bropenscience is broken science, *The Psychologist*, 33: 34–7.

Wicherts, J.M., Borsboom, D., Kats, J. and Molenaar, D. (2006). The poor availability of psychological research data for reanalysis, *American Psychologist*, 61: 726–8. Available at https://doi.org/10.1037/0003-066X.61.7.726 (accessed 31 August 2022).

Wicherts, J.M., Veldkamp, C.L.S., Augusteijn, H.E., Bakker, M., van Aert, R.C.M. and van Assen, M.A.L.M. (2016). Degrees of freedom in planning, running, analyzing, and reporting psychological studies: A checklist to avoid *p*-hacking, *Frontiers in Psychology*, 7: 1832. Available at https://dx.doi.org/10.3389%2Ffpsyg.2016.01832 (accessed 31 August 2022).

Wiggins, B.J. and Christopherson, C.D. (2019). The replication crisis in psychology: An overview for theoretical and philosophical psychology, *Journal of Theoretical & Philosophical Psychology*, 39: 202–17. Available at https://doi.org/10.1037/teo0000137 (accessed 31 August 2022).

Wilkinson, M., Dumontier, M., Aalbersberg, I. et al. (2016). The FAIR Guiding Principles for scientific data management and stewardship, *Scientific Data*, 3: 160018. Available at https://doi.org/10.1038/sdata.2016.18 (accessed 31 August 2022).

Wiseman, R., Watt, C. and Kornbrot, D. (2019). Registered Reports: An early example and analysis, *PeerJ*, 7: e6232. Available at http://doi.org/10.7717/peerj.6232 (accessed 31 August 2022).

Xu, X., Demos, K.E., Leahey, T.M. et al. (2014). Failure to replicate depletion of self-control, *PLoS One*, 9: e109950. Available at https://doi.org/10.1371/journal.pone.0109950 (accessed 31 August 2022).

Yarkoni, T. (2013). What we can and can't learn from the Many Labs Replication Project, *Talyarkoni.org* [blog], 27 December. Available at https://www.talyarkoni.org/blog/2013/12/27/what-we-can-and-cant-learn-from-the-many-labs-replication-project/ (accessed 31 August 2022).

Zarin, D.A. and Keselman, A. (2007). Registering a clinical trial in ClinicalTrials.gov, *Chest*, 131: 909–12. Available at https://doi.org/10.1378/chest.06-2450 (accessed 31 August 2022).

Zarin, D.A., Tse, T., Williams, R.J. and Rajakannan, T. (2017). Update on trial registration 11 years after the ICMJE policy was established, *New England Journal of Medicine*, 376: 383–91. Available at https://doi.org/10.1056/NEJMsr1601330 (accessed 31 August 2022).

Zečević, K., Houghton, C., Noone, C., Lee, H., Matvienko-Sikar, K. and Toomey, E. (2021). Exploring factors that influence the practice of Open Science by early career health researchers: A mixed methods study, *HRB Open Research*, 3: 56. Available at https://doi.org/10.12688/hrbopenres.13119.2 (accessed 31 August 2022).

Ziano, I., Yan Mok, P. and Feldman, G. (2021). Replication and extension of Alicke (1985) better-than-average effect for desirable and controllable traits, *Social Psychological & Personality Science*, 12: 1005–17. Available at https://doi.org/10.1177%2F1948550620948973 (accessed 31 August 2022).

Zigerell, L.J. (2017). Potential publication bias in the stereotype threat literature: Comment on Nguyen and Ryan (2008), *Journal of Applied Psychology*, 1–2: 1159–68. Available at https://doi.org/10.1037/apl0000188 (accessed 31 August 2022).

Zou, C.X., Becker, J.E., Phillips, A.T. et al. (2018). Registration, results reporting, and publication bias of clinical trials supporting FDA approval of neuropsychiatric drugs before and after FDAAA: A retrospective cohort study, *Trials*, 19: 581. Available at https://doi.org/10.1186/s13063-018-2957-0 (accessed 31 August 2022).

Glossary

Below are definitions of the terms highlighted in bold and italics throughout this book. In addition, I recommend the excellent glossary of open scholarship terms by Parsons et al.:

Parsons, S., Azevedo, F., Elsherif, M. M. et al. (2022). A community-sourced glossary of open scholarship terms. *Nature Human Behaviour*, 6: 312–18. https://doi.org/10.1038/s41562-021-01269-4. Available at: https://forrt.org/glossary/open-access/

Apophenia: Our natural predisposition to notice patterns in random data and our preference for positive over negative findings.

A priori: Based on theoretical deduction rather than empirical observation.

Big team science: Open, large-scale collaboration between researchers who work together to solve fundamental research questions and pool resources across different labs, institutions, disciplines, cultures and continents (Forscher et al. 2022; Lieck, 2022).

Citation bias: The tendency to disproportionately cite positive compared to null results (de Vries et al., 2018).

Cognitive biases: A systematic error in thinking that occurs when people interpret the world around them. This affects judgement and decision-making.

Conceptual replication: Using a different set of methods and/or measures that test the same hypotheses.

Confidence interval (CI): A range of values that is likely to include a population value with a certain degree of confidence. It is often expressed as a percentage, whereby a population mean lies between an upper and lower interval.

Confirmation bias: The tendency to search for or interpret information in a manner that supports our existing beliefs (Mahoney, 1977).

Confirmatory research: The process of testing a specific hypothesis, informed by theory, to measure the strength of evidence using pre-specified analyses. This is sometimes known as 'hypothesis-testing' research.

Construct validity: Whether a measure 'behaves' in a way consistent with theoretical hypotheses (Cronbach and Meehl, 1955; Fink, 2010).

Data codebook: A list and detailed annotation of all of the variables in a data set, what they refer to and how they were compiled. Also known as a 'data dictionary'.

Effect size: A quantitative measure of the magnitude of an experimental effect. Examples include correlation coefficients (Pearson's r) and differences between means (Cohen's d). One advantage is that, unlike p-values, effect sizes are independent of sample size.

Exact replication: Using the exact same methods and/or measures as an original study. The replication study should be as close to the original as possible. Also known as 'direct replication'.

Exploratory research: The process of exploring or uncovering relationships between variables without any prior assumptions or hypotheses or by running different analyses. This is sometimes referred to as 'hypothesis-generating' research.

External validity: Whether the results of an original study can be generalized to other contexts and/or populations (Cook and Campbell, 1979).

False positive: The incorrect rejection of a null hypothesis. In other words, finding a significant result by chance when the null hypothesis is true. This is also known as a Type I error.

False negative: The incorrect rejection of the experimental hypothesis. In other words, finding a non-significant result by chance when the alternative hypothesis is true. This is also known as a Type II error.

Falsification: The ability to disprove a proposition, hypothesis or theory. Popper (2002 [1959]) suggests that for a theory and its hypothesis to be considered scientific it must be able to be tested and conceivably proven false. For example, the hypothesis that 'all swans are white' can be falsified by observing a black swan.

File drawer problem: The phenomenon whereby studies with null or inconclusive results are never published and have no findable documentation (Rosenthal, 1979).

Hindsight bias: The tendency to see an event or finding as predictable only *after* it has occurred.

Hypothesizing After Results are Known (HARKing): A questionable research practice that occurs when a researcher changes their experimental hypothesis after looking at the direction of their results (Kerr, 1998).

Internal validity: How a study establishes a cause-and-effect relationship between the independent and dependent variables (Cook and Campbell, 1979).

Lindley's paradox: Describes the paradox that in very large sample sizes, p-values around the .05 region (e.g. $p = .04$) can actually indicate support for the null hypothesis (Lindley, 1957).

Meta-analysis: A statistical analysis that combines the results of multiple scientific studies. One goal of a meta-analysis is to estimate an overall, or combined, effect. The accuracy of this pooled 'effect size estimate' is dependent on the accuracy of studies that are included in the meta-analysis.

Meta-research: Research into how researchers do research. Also known as 'meta-science'.

Null finding(s): The outcome of a null significance hypothesis test (NHST) indicates that there is no significant effect, or relationship, between variables. This is also referred to as a 'null result' or 'null effect'.

Open access (OA): The free, public availability of a research product on the internet for distribution and reuse with acknowledgment. OA is typically used in reference to published journal articles, but any output could be OA, including student works and study materials, code and data (Crüwell et al., 2019).

Open code: Making computer code (e.g. programming, analysis code) publicly available to make research methodology and analysis transparent and to facilitate reproducibility.

Open data: Making data publicly available for viewing, reproducing and reuse. Open data must uphold ethical considerations (e.g. participant anonymity). Also known as 'data sharing'.

Open materials: Making study materials (e.g. questionnaires, experimental tasks, interviews) publicly available to facilitate reproducibility and reuse.

Open science: An umbrella term reflecting the idea that knowledge should be openly accessible, transparent, rigorous, reproducible, replicable and inclusive.

Optional stopping: A questionable research practice where a researcher repeatedly analyses their data during ongoing data collection and purposely decides to stop when the p-value reaches a desired threshold (e.g. $p < .05$).

PhD: Short for 'Doctor of Philosophy', an academic or professional degree that involves students conducting a series of research studies that are bound into a written thesis.

Preprint: A scientific document made available legally outside of a traditional publisher by posting it online in a trusted internet repository (e.g. PsyArXiv).

Preregistration: Registering a study protocol, including the research questions, hypotheses, design, variables and data analysis plan before data collection and/or analysis.

Publication bias: A phenomenon in which significant/positive results are favoured and published in higher quantities than non-significant, or undesirable results.

Peer review: A system used to assess the quality of a manuscript before it is published. Experts in the relevant research field evaluate the manuscript and provide feedback to help journal editors determine whether a manuscript should be published in the journal.

P-HACKing: A questionable research practice which describes the many ways in which a researcher can obtain a statistically significant result.

P-value: The probability of the observed or more extreme data, under the assumption that the null hypothesis is true (Fisher 1934, 1955).

Qualitative research: The process of collecting, analysing and interpreting non-numerical data (e.g. text, images, video) to explore experiences in depth.

Quantitative research: The process of collecting, analysing and interpreting numerical data with the use of statistics.

Questionable Measurement Practices (QMPs): The nondisclosure of validity when such estimates are found to be unsatisfactory.

Questionable Research Practices (QRPs): An umbrella term referring to a range of behaviours that researchers can engage in, either intentionally or unintentionally, to distort their findings (Parsons et al. 2022).

Registered Report: A publishing format where initial peer review is performed on a study protocol before data collection and/or analyses are conducted. Peer review is split into two stages: pre-study (Stage 1) and post-study (Stage 2). Accepted Stage 1 manuscripts are given 'in principle acceptance' (IPA), moving the focus to the process of research and away from the results.

Registered Replication Report (RRR): A type of research study which combines the results of multiple independently conducted replication attempts of an original study, following a detailed and vetted protocol.

Replicability: Obtaining consistent results across studies or experiments aimed at answering the same scientific question, each of which has obtained its own data.

Replication crisis: A problem in both psychology and many other disciplines in which scientific findings are difficult or impossible to reproduce or replicate. Also known as the 'reproducibility crisis' and 'credibility revolution'.

Reproducibility: Obtaining consistent results using the same input data and analysis techniques.

Scientific method: An empirical method of acquiring knowledge that has characterized the development of science since the fifteenth century (Sir Francis Bacon, 1561–1626) to provide logical, rational problem solving across scientific fields.

Secondary data analyses: The analysis of existing data to investigate research questions in addition to the main ones for which the data were originally collected (Grady et al. 2013; van den Akker et al. 2021a).

Statistical power: The long-run probability that a statistical test correctly rejects the null hypothesis if the alternative/experimental hypothesis is true.

Statistical significance: A property of a result using NHST that, given a significance level, is deemed unlikely to have occurred given the null hypothesis. This is based on *p*-values.

Index